FINDING SUPERHERO
IN
Havana

A MEMOIR

ORLANDO GARCIA-PIEDRA MD

Professional Acknowledgements

Cover and design
Jesús Cordero: Anointing Productions
Website: www.anointingproductions.com
Email: jesuscorder@gmail.com
Cover based on inspiration of derivative work, similar but
not identical, of photograph on page 95 in book Six Days
in Havana by James A. Michener and John Kings. First
Edition 1989. University of Texas Press, Box 7819. Austin Tx
78713-7819

Editing
Katherine Pickett POP Editorial Services, LLC 11003
Lombardy Road Silver Spring, MD 20901
Website: www.PopEditing.net
Email: Katherine@popediting.net

Publishing and Publicist
Steve Harrison, owner - Bradley Communications Corp.
Havertown, PA Coaches: - Geoffrey Berwind - Debbie
Englander - Cristina Smith - Raia King
Website: www.steveharrison.com
Email: Email@authorsuccess.com

Printing, Marketing, Distribution, and Self-Publishing
IngramSpark
Website: www.ingramspark.com
Email: info@ingramspark.com

Dedication

Licinio **Humberto** (Gallego) **Garcia Perez**

Some kids dream their lives, then work to live their dream. It helps when you have good friends and a supporting family to walk the trail with you, applaud and savor the victories, or wipe away, with sweat in their hands, the lonely tears of loss or defeat. It is here and now that I drop to my knees to give thanks for the blessing of having a story to write and the time to write it.

This one is for you, Dad

Narrative

FOLLOWS THE 10 MOST RELEVANT DAYS IN MY LIFE

"The most amazing day" August 1946. My birth.

"The most surprising day" August 1956. My sister's birth.

"The most exciting day" Summer 1957. I first saw
Yankee Stadium.

"The happiest day" December 1958. Return from Palm Beach.

"The most important day" January 1959. Escape from Havana.

"The most embarrassing day" February 1959. I drop a dinner
tray on the teacher's wife.

"The most incredible day" Winter 1961. I find my dogs.

"The luckiest day" Spring 1964. I meet Mary Carmen.

"The most disappointing day" Christmas 1965.

Madeline's last love letter.

"The saddest day" May 1967. I lose my father.

Content

Cuba

Exile

Characters

Main Characters

Orlando (The author: Superman)
Orlando (The child: Superboy)
God (The co-author)
Humberto (Orlando's Brother)
Humberto's Ghost
Mother's Ghost
Dad's Ghost

Secondary Characters

Rita (maternal grandmother)
Esperanza (paternal grandmother)
Madeline (1st girlfriend)
Mary Carmen (2nd girlfriend)
Ana Maria (Orlando's sister)
Aunt Chely (Tía Tá)
Uncle Orlando Piedra (Cuban FBI Chief)
René (Lex Luthor)

Preface

*F*INDING *S*UPERHERO IN *H*AVANA IS A CHILDHOOD MEMOIR written in the style of a fantasy novel, about a kid looking for his alter ego, "Superboy," and an adult, "Superman," looking for his family---now physically departed but spiritually present as forces---ghosts animating his life. This is also a spiritual journey, that explains how God's resurrection induce possibilities for his ancestry and brother to survive bodily death to reappear as ghosts, becoming a positive influence in his journey. Their actions today portray a generous spirit marked by enthusiasm, kindness, and courage.

Do I really believe in ghosts? Of course, I do, well beyond and far surpassing my often fractured fragile "reality." My ghosts helped me write this memoir, especially at night camouflaged by darkness. What a blast meeting all the ghosts from my past! I was scared but felt excited to tell others what happened to me, hoping my accomplishments and failures would help guide someone else's journey.

Do I really believe in God? Again, I say, of course I do, well beyond and far surpassing my often fractured, fragile "reality." Throughout the tale, I challenge the Creator to explain my journey as well as that of my ghosts. Herein lies the struggle of Superboy vs God. To clarify ideas, I asked God to be *coauthor*. He accepted. I became attached to Him. Everyone is attached to something or someone, until we are not. Multiple attachments and detachments defined my life course, explained through moments in time, lived during impacting days I recall.

For an individual to have a good life or to have one that is worth living, Socrates maintained, he must be a critical questioner or must have an interrogative soul. Socrates established the importance of asking deep questions that probe profoundly into thinking before we accept ideas as worthy of belief. Thus, my purpose became elucidating some truths about the events that formed the memories, then transcribe their content to a philosophy of reason in order to help others. It appeared complicated.

At seventy-four, my past is convoluted, as images blur and possibilities feel endless. What did I hear and see that was so remarkable and noteworthy? I searched for memories from the most important day in my life, noon, New Year's Eve, 1958 through midnight, New Year's Day, 1959—-a 36-hour day. It became a new beginning. I was twelve.

I searched again for why I should embark on this endeavor and I realized *respect* is what I really wanted as a child, and still do. But even more vitally important was to tell the story of my family. I thought, "I will show everyone what a great family I had, and who I was and became."

And then I stumbled. I remember being a good kid, funny and wholesome but concerned about his self-image. Wishing to portray my childhood in a good light, I resolved:

"I'm going to look good no matter what."

I wanted to show off my amazing childhood. So, I created a stunning synoptic outline of *me*, like a pyramid with a "super me," *Superboy*, at the top, everyone, and everything else below building up my superpower one block at a time.

I realized my new job, authoring my first book, could be as exciting as I wanted; only I would ever know if something was true or false, unless I told you. Thus, I chose to tell my "stories" colored by my perceptions, choosing the *happiest day?* The *saddest day?* The *luckiest day?* Now, I had a method to relate my childhood to extraordinary characters or challenging times or stressful situations. Love, hate, racism, fear, family, politics, social change, sex, and baseball mattered most. They make my memoir real.

But I began to get concerned. I needed one thing to cement everything else: *confidence.* Suddenly, I heard Him deep inside, as His voice kept creeping up...

"Orlando, Orlando, listen to me."
"Oh, my God!" I exclaimed, full of fear and astonishment.
"You must tell the truth," He said.
"Yes, I promise never to lie," I replied.

I assured Him: "The story I will write is a tale of things [that] and people [who] became part of my life. I promise to tell the truth." Then, I lied. I struggled with divulging my truth.

Knowing the totality of the work must make sense, I indulged in *critical thinking.* Spiritual and religious reasoning appeared to have had a major impact. Searching for events relevant to my world before and after that most important day, I recalled reading *Superman* comics. I dreamed the story of myself as someone I was not, a superhero, amazing, daring, and full of life and death-relevant events. The main character (Superboy) was not even going to be me!

The fictional superhero was born on the planet Krypton and named Kal-El. As a baby, he was sent to Earth in a small spaceship by his scientist father Jor-El moments before Krypton was destroyed in a natural cataclysm. His ship landed in the American (Kansas) countryside; he was found by a passing motorist and adopted by farmers Jonathan and Martha Kent, who named him *Clark Kent.*

Displaying superhuman abilities, such as incredible strength and impervious skin, he was advised by his foster parents to fight for the benefit of humanity. He decides to battle crime as a vigilante. To protect his privacy, now a reporter for The Daily News he changes into a colorful costume and uses the alias <Superman> when fighting crime.

Clark Kent moves from Smallville, his hometown, to Metropolis to attend journalism school. He wears glasses as a disguise for his civilian identity.

Superboy's adventures include the story of how he reunited with his super dog, Krypto; how his friend, the teenage scientist Lex Luthor, becomes his most bitter foe; and how he joins the thirtieth-century Legion of Super-Heroes.

Searching for the connection between me, the main character, and my favored superhero, I reasoned his incorporation into my autobiography by contemplating a list of a superhero's amazing feats, strengths, and weaknesses. I wondered: What desirable superhero characteristics exist? I self-analyzed. I owned a few.

To be truthful, I lacked courage, physical strength, self-respect, determination, and capacity (I had the desire) to protect the world. I recall being open-minded, curious, and creative, in love with my surroundings. I lacked bravery and leadership. I was honest, loving, and kind, but lacked prudence, humility, and forgiveness. I was humorous, analytical, empathic, and harmonious, a dreamer, but lacked self-regulation and intellect. In spite of all the negatives, I was finding superhero. It all began to unfold as I created my main character.

I did not disguise in a superhero costume, was not able to achieve the speed of light, nor wore eyeglasses, and my 20/20 Cuban childhood vision was incapable of infrared heat power. But I "saw and heard" a world unseen and unheard by others. Thankfully, my Ma and Pa were not foster parents. I doubt to reach the thirtieth century, and Havana was no Smallville. I grew up within a politically powerful SUPER family, in neighborhoods filled with everything any kid could ever want or wish to have or dream to own.

Still, I did not know where to begin. Searching for facts, I began a conversation with myself.

Orlando--- I am not certain about God's existence; how can I be certain about anything?

Superboy--- I know all living things, including humans, can trace their beginning to a common ancestor, God, or a monkey if you are an atheist. Attachment to Him is a choice, as it is to deny creation and embrace evolution. I know you will make the correct choice: Believe in Him.

Orlando--- You are my superhero. To tell my story, I need to find you!

It was getting a bit crazy...I asked God for help.

Orlando--- God, would you, could you, will you please be my coauthor? I need your power to find my truth!

God--- All right, let us summarize. You were born in Cuba, from white parents also born there, their parents' direct descendants of Spanish *conquistadores*. Research your ancestry. This is your autobiography. You must find out where and who you come from.

Orlando--- let's do this.

CUBA
Part 1

──────────•──────────

And So, It Begins

[2017]

Chapter 1
A Child's Story

PERMÍTAME PRESENTARME. ME LLAMO ORLANDO.

On a Saturday morning in early 2017, around 5 am, I sat down on a comfortable couch in the living room and began writing. "I am… dramatic, dynamic, *'culo inquieto'* (restless ass), *emprendedor* (enterprising), a risk taker, a dreamer, etc." About two hours later, my wife, Mary Carmen woke up and joined me.

Mary Carmen--- You are up early.
Orlando--- I am writing. I started my book.

I asked her for guidance---which I do often. She smiled.

Mary Carmen--- Do not use your work to air grievances, settle scores, or feed resentments. Is it in English or Spanish?
Orlando--- Are you being facetious?
Mary Carmen--- No [white lie].
Orlando--- Both. It will be authentic, a documentary with no holds barred. I will be truthful to myself in a style compatible to my personality, in line with the child I was, the world I experienced and those who shared it, and leave out details that could shame or injure anyone's reputation.

Knowing my promise was somewhat unreal, she gave me "the look."

Orlando--- Please, describe me in your own words.

Mary Carmen--- You are thoughtful, a worrier, family-oriented, take-no-prisoners ruthless.

Orlando--- Like Stalin, Lenin, Hitler?

She smiled again. I know I can count on that smile. It is not a must for success, but it helps. I told her God had written me a letter.

Mary Carmen--- What?

Orlando--- For starters, God told me, "you must decide where you will begin your story." So, I listened closely, to seek His Truth as guidance. After all, He is my coauthor.

Mary Carmen--- What?

Orlando--- He said, "Each chapter must be meaningful, tell the truth, and flow"...He would not have it any other way.

I really needed help. Wishing for inspiration, I realized I was listening to a song, interpreted by Belgian singer, Donna Winner, "One Moment in Time." The last verse:

"Give me one moment in time
When I'm more than I thought I could be
When all of my dreams are a heartbeat away
And the answers are all up to me
Give me one moment in time
When I'm racing with destiny
Then, in that one moment of time, I will be,
I will be free."
---John Bettis and Albert Hammond.

Orlando--- That's it! I will seek, retrieve, and write relevant moments in time, then, I will be free!

Conscious of being too serious or boring, I promised myself to have fun while I wrote. Searching again for the right way to start my tale, ideas began to clear. Then, reality hit. I do not remember what I did yesterday; how will I recall sixty years ago?

I tried to make some sense of blurred memories clinging to the sadness borne from personal loss, carried daily in my bones. Eyes watered.

This prompted a search for the science of memory and child psychology [interesting]. I had to find some help [difficult], read autobiographies [boring], spend many hours sitting [impossible], and beg my wife [easy] to read [challenging] or to listen [intolerable] to what I wrote.

The book's format is weird. It is written in conversational English and Spanish, simply because I am bilingual. Comments from me and conversations between characters appear simultaneously. As I wrote the outline, I thought, my God, what a mess!

Wisely, God stepped in to fix everything.

God--- Your signifiers deal with human rupture, racism, justice, generational fragmentation of most of a country's population, financial disaster, family separation, hunger, and death. After arriving in the United States, you and your family saw opportunities for financial success, family reunification, continuing education, and better health. Correct?

Orlando--- Yes, the dream of again gaining access to the possibility of reopening our hearts to You, through both victory and defeat; regaining our humanity as foundation for hope, faith, and love, particularly amongst those who reached freedom.

God--- So it was not all bad.
Orlando--- I did not say it was.

Failing to hold back my tears, I began to cry; all I could think about was the day we left Cuba, never to return. It was the first time I saw my parents' pain and suffering, with their injured confidence exposed, and their fear and helplessness scared the hell out of me.

Losing everything, my world turned upside down, a dichotomy appeared: A huge loss (Cuba) turns into a bigger gain---*Freedom.*

Orlando--- *¡Pepe! ¡Ven! ¡Juguemos a los escondidos!* (Come on, Pepe, let us play hide-and-seek!)
Pepe--- *Ya voy* (I'm coming.)
Orlando--- *¡René! ¡Vístete! ¡Mamá nos va a llevar a comer helado!* (René! get dressed! Mom's going to take us for ice cream!)
René--- *Ya voy* (I'm coming.)

Looking within, seeking truth, I see more than one person---actually three: a weak kid, a strong kid, and an adult kid manipulating the first two. I have realized something amazing, totally new to my self-image. I owned a triple personality: The Good, The Bad, and The Ugly.

Orlando is the writer, the author of the story of the kid I was, too often self-imaged as "the ugly" and scared of each new experience but willing to give living a shot.

Superboy was my superhero, an imaginary alter ego, owning an outstanding self-image: the fabulous, daring, powerful, and yet kind child, "the good" I dreamed to be.

Humberto, my brother, "the bad" know-it-all, fearless "grownup" became the third part of who I was. We had a love-hate relationship.

Mother (Superwoman) encouraged me to believe I was Superboy, so I set out to become a superhero. Me and mom were close. She was like God, omniscient, omnipotent, and omnipresent, capable of having an eternal and necessary existence. Both she and Dad were my superheroes.

Every new experience impacted survival learning, exactly as both parents intended it would. Leaning on their strong leadership, I found my support, especially from Mom, as Chona (mom's nickname) exampled mental strength and moral fortitude, mapping the road to follow.

Other mothers in the family led likewise: Rita Piedra, Mom's mom; Esperanza Pérez, Dad's mom; and Aunt Chely (Tía Tá), Dad's sister.

With each new encounter, I thought, a friend or a foe? A good thing or a bad thing? A helper or a disabler? A win to later celebrate or a loss to regret? As I found my characters and built my personality, I adopted this meaning-making behavior into my persona, mirroring role models, or the opposite, rejecting them. I also sensed a growing attachment to my brother, Humberto.

God--- Don't worry, Superboy. Together, we will get it done.

Chapter 2
A Letter from God

Dear Orlando,

You are not Superman, nor where you ever Superboy. Your problem is believing that you were and are superhuman. I am the only superhuman entity in both the planet and the universe. I was human, once, through my son, and his name was Jesus. What, in My Name, are you doing? Who do you think you are?

My life's work was man's salvation. There is no gift greater than you. I spent thirty-three years worrying about you, and now I feel good seeing your commitment to me. Although, I must say, you fall prey to Satan too often. You were a weak child, and now you are a weak adult.

Don't stop loving yourself, because then I will not feel your love for me. Don't stop working on behalf of your brothers and sisters, for that will make my day a lot busier. Don't cry me a river of tears from pain, disappointments, and struggle, because my cup runneth over with the oceans from victims' blood, sweat, and tears shed while trying to survive famine, ethnic cleansing, mass homicide, poverty, child trafficking, illicit drugs, and suicide.

Please understand my predicament. I do have empathy, and feel you are now on the right track to where you think you must go. But don't despair, all you have to do is trust me.

Heavenly yours,
God

Chapter 3
My Language

My first five years of life were especially critical as I matured through phases during which I explored my environment. I also learned verbal and reasoning skills, socialized with others, and, eventually, asserted my dream for independence. Prioritizing my safety and fruitful development, my family and I spent most of this time in a suburb of Havana called, *La Víbora,* (The Viper).

I was late to begin talking, but once I started, it became difficult to stop me. Research found similarities of language acquisition across cultures and has discerned how parents communicate with babies to help them develop new vocabulary.

My mother loved to tell the story of what appeared to be an expressive language impairment disorder that made it hard for me to find the right words and form clear sentences when speaking. The way I verbalized the word for "orange" *(naranja)* was "*cherna*" because this fruit originated in China and I probably heard it as *"naranja China,"* pronounced "cheena" in Spanish. To this day, Mother speaks to me about how to express myself.

Mom's Ghost--- You are writing a book. Tell me more about your style. Will it be clear in delivering content, flowing through simple ideas expressed in words easy to read and understand? I suggest using definitions of words and quotes, and music lyrics you find fundamental, to improve reader understanding; I mean, for the reader to follow your train of thought.

Orlando--- Yes, Mom, that is exactly what I am doing. I mean, what "we" are doing.

Mom's Ghost--- What do you mean, "we?"

God--- I am his coauthor.

Dad's Ghost--- My God! I cannot wait to read it.

Orlando--- There is so much I have learned! Stuff I never dreamed existed.

Dad's Ghost--- Your language in this book promises to be complicated, but also deep and interesting.

God--- Some words are more meaningful than others. The meaning of the words we use relates to their significance as to our capacity to retrieve them from accessible memory. The quality of Orlando's relationships, the confidence with which he lived his young life, and the difference he made in the lives of others became his enjoyment of life, all dreams sprouting as I watched all of you develop as a family. He will become a conscientious writer.

The pressure Mother exerted on me as I wrote became a source of concern. How could I craft a language her ghost could, should, or would accept? Her influence on my early life was significant, as she used persuasion and intimidation when guiding my development, like a bully demanding lunch money from a student, or the student gets beaten.

Mother always reminded us that "family is the mirror upon which we present our image for approval." She would say, "Just know this, when you tell everyone about you and your family, pay close attention to the information divulged, or pay the consequences."

Her parenting philosophy was not geared toward accepting her children as who we were, instead leaning more toward guiding us to become "normal" adults---that is, *en su imágen y semejanza* (in her image and likeness). She stressed normal behavior as that which followed identical principles to those taught and demanded by her parents, Rita, and José, as she and her siblings grew up in Cuba.

Dad's ghost, on the other hand, exerted no pressure whatsoever when I began to disclose my interest in writing my story. Thanks to his job as senior customs officer, both at Havana's Harbor and its International Rancho Bolleros "José Martí" Airport, Dad was a "world traveler" without leaving the island. His education grew with various non-Hispanic words; foreigners he met enriched his business language, providing resources Mom lacked.

Although on the surface it appeared that he was not too concerned regarding the content of my story or the way I was writing it, his sole presence provided comfort as I listened with great interest and focused attention to everything he said and everything I saw him do or heard he did.

Mom's Ghost--- Son, whatever you are going to "remember" when you write, this story better be good and decent. I mean, I would not write anything bad about your family.

Mom kept reminding me to "keep it clean," light, and not too funny, and most of all "respectful" so that she would not be embarrassed. She stressed I should not dwell too much on family connections.

Orlando--- Mom, your soul is in Heaven now; be happy and stop worrying about my troubles as a writer. I am trying to figure out my childhood, and you happen to be in it.

Mom's Ghost--- It is alarming. Just do not repeat what you heard at home.

The Piedras worked in government, holding key leadership positions in a country at war. Mom did not want to reveal government secrets I heard during adult conversations.

Orlando--- Mom, I am just trying to be me, an authentic old man, writing about the authentic child in his memory. One of my biggest challenges is judging others.

Mom's Ghost--- Concurrently, you were also judged.

God--- Judging new acquaintances and family members became a staple of growing up but did not help your relationships; the real became fantasy as you "classified" people into drawers and boxes.

Mom's Ghost--- Judging persons does not define who *they* are, it defines who *you* are.

God--- When you pass judgment, you express your strong disapproval of someone or something. If you're overly critical of your job, a family member, a neighbor, or even yourself, you tend to criticize every little nuisance.

Dad's Ghost--- The worst thing about people who pass judgment on others is that they tend to act morally superior, as if they're in a position to judge the actions of other people.

Orlando--- Sometimes, I find myself yelling at another driver on the road for aggressive driving behavior. Knowing I do the same thing, it is clear I need to look at my own behavior before passing judgement.

Dad's Ghost--- You must be careful not to judge someone who does not appear to you as intelligent, competent, kind, or able to provide services as efficiently as you. He or she may be solving a problem in a different way than you would. Or maybe they have a different timetable than you do.

Orlando--- I must confess: Truths and fantasies impacting my development proved intimidating until resolved to my satisfaction, as I built *confidence* toward becoming well-adjusted and balanced.

Dad's Ghost--- I trust you, son. I am confident your language will mirror perceptions derived from those truths and fantasies, achieving knowledge you will transfer to your memoir.

God--- Your younger years presented challenges. Resolving each one, enriched your personal and unique "accessible" memory. Other issues did not resolve, becoming a "storage" failure.

Orlando--- You are right. My language is limited to personal knowledge. I probably still reject those failures, holding on to pleasant memories while discarding painful events.

There are many things that I knew I knew: how I got my name, who taught me to drive a car, to read, to walk. The best baseball players on earth. My fears and bad dreams, like the one about Humberto drowning. We were both *in* the ocean and I tried hard to save him, but I could not. He drowned.

Dad's Ghost--- You may not wish to share a painful experience from your accessible memory. I know you are scared. Do not worry; you'll be all right. Remain truthful and honest to yourself and everyone else.

Orlando--- Easier said than done. Truth is hard to live with and share, so we lie to ourselves and others. Honesty is hard to find because it is hard to give.

"It is such a lonely word, because it's hardly ever heard." Billy Joel wrote that. "It's no wonder that truth is stranger than fiction. Fiction has to make sense." That's Mark Twain.

Orlando--- Yes, it is, Billy, and, yes it does, Mark. Absolute truth is unreal; it flows from the subconscious. Kids and crazies never lie. Children build denial as they develop into their adult selves. Personal "realities" are kept by children as absolute truths to later enjoy, as adults, as their fantasy. Truth is what you want it to be.

Who is us? Who are we? Who was I? According to Freud, I was three:

Orlandito (Little Orlando), the *"Id"*---my most primitive animal nature.

Superboy, the *"Superego"*---the kid I wanted to be, in tune with a system of judgements imposed by the society I longed to be a part of.

Orlando, the *"Ego"*---the troubled soul attempting to balance himself by accommodating the other two.

I write this tale using a language that will expose my transformation from Orlandito, through Superboy, to Orlando (Superman). The multiple mirrors positioned in different angles to my vision, reflect that conversion which informs the story.

Unbeknownst to me at the time, everyone I knew during my childhood was racist, even my grandmothers---Esperanza and Rita---the sweetest people in the world. For them, it did not have to make sense to accept racism; it was already the centuries-old "law of the land" in plain view. It was something they knew that they knew, and they talked about it with certainty and righteousness that it was God-given to be white and rich or black and poor, in wealth and education, or in its lack, in health and access to it, or in its absence, and in the right to socially mingle or rejection.

They could be honest [truthful] without feeling guilt. They perceived racism only in others, negating its existence within themselves. It all seemed reasonable in the context of the times. No different from my white-only friends. I saw nothing wrong with it.

As society progressed and new demands for human rights appeared, no one in the family initially supported blacks' rights to assemble in private clubs, hotels, and schools, but never felt offended by those who accessed "our" world. I never heard anyone in my family speak of "them" derogatorily. I do not recall a single offensive comment, a racist remark; but no one talked about their progress, their plight, fearing conflictive views borne from prejudice would bring a negative light upon them.

* * * * *

Dad's Ghost--- Orlando, get in touch with your inner child. Do not worry about your mother's or your brother's ghosts. You can be yourself only if you allow others to be themselves. Follow your intuition. Pray to your coauthor to strengthen your resolve to remain authentic.

God--- Orlando, I will help you fight denial of your truth in order for you to learn who you really were.

Superboy--- Orlando, you must remain clear-minded and courageous to transcribe your reality to your work.

Orlando--- Thanks to all three of you. Just help me keep Mom and Humberto at bay.

Chapter 4
Naming a Newborn

Sometime during the month of February 1946, my infant brother, Humberto, interrupted a family conversation at my parents' apartment in Old Havana. The family reunion was arranged by Mother to announce she was pregnant and to request input in naming me. By the end of the day, they had "Orlando" as first choice. *Humbertico* (small Humberto) was needing a diaper change.

Spanish naming customs provide for a given name followed by two surnames: First, the father's and second, the mother's. All paternal family names (García for me) plus the maternal family name (Piedra) were kept in ecclesiastical records at the local parish. With Baptism, a third name was added, similar to a middle name in the US--- though not necessarily baptismal. In my case, my parents added "de Jesús"---i.e., belonging to Jesus---to my name. Planned before I was born, that is how I became Orlando de Jesús García Piedra.

Mom's Ghost--- This system guaranteed all my children, Humberto, Ana Maria, and you, to keep both of your parents' family names, Garcia and Piedra, following civil law, while still keeping with Catholic dogma of Baptism, for the course of a lifetime.

She was right, but only true for men. For women, it was true only while still single. Later in life, with marriage, the husband

[Dad] would keep both his paternal family name (García) and maternal family name (Pérez), while the wife [Mom] kept only her paternal family name (Piedra). She "lost" her maternal name (Negueruela) and, in its place, added the preposition "de" (of) following her family name, Piedra: Oraida Piedra *de* Garcia.

By preceding Dad's family name (García), the word "de" implied she literally identified as socially belonging to Dad. Used only in social conversation, this male tradition was meant and forwarded as a sexist belief women were born to serve men, de facto approving excessive or prejudiced loyalty to a husband as the "natural" way to behave. It showed male strength and power.

Orlando---Already a fetus, before my birth, I belonged to Jesus Christ. My name was unofficially Orlando. Then, at Baptism you added "de Jesus." I had no idea naming someone was that complicated.

Mom's Ghost--- Everything seemed complicated to you because you were just a child.

Orlando--- So, Mom, you kept your family name (Piedra) but followed it with "de García," implying you belonged to Dad. And that was forever, was it not?

Dad's Ghost--- Oraida Piedra *de* García.

Dad flashed a mischievous grin.

Orlando--- Why did she have to lose her mother's family name? Did you consider her a slave or something? Did you think you owned her?

Dad's Ghost--- A sign of the times and the place, thankfully no longer true in most households.

Orlando--- Why was "Orlando" chosen?

Mother's Ghost--- Choosing a name is a very personal experience.

Esperanza's Ghost--- *Por tradición, yo, tu abuela paterna, tenía el derecho de escoger el nombre de mis nietos primero, o por lo menos retener la voz cantante en la decisión final.* (By tradition, I, as your paternal grandmother, had first choice of naming all grandchildren or at least placing a heavy hand on the final decision.)

However, Uncle Orlando (Landín), considered the *padrino* (godfather) by all in the family, was politically exiled in Miami following Batista's first presidential mandate. During that time, his life was at risk. So, Mom offered the Virgin Mary to name me after her brother with the spiritual implication of Heavenly protection.

Orlando--- I was Orlando, but also "Gallego." Humberto called me that.

Superboy--- So, who named you, I mean, us?

Orlando--- Sorry, Superboy. I don't mean to upset you, but I'm the one who gave you your name. I am writing this story, in which you appear a few years after my birth. That is when I named you. I'm trying to find out who named me.

Esperanza's Ghost--- *Ya os lo dije. Yo fuí.* (I already told you. I did.)

Mom's Ghost--- *No, Esperanza, Usted no fué. Yo nombré a Orlandito con el nombre de Landín.* (No, Esperanza. You did not. I named Orlandito after Landín.)

Orlando--- Please take me out of my misery.

Mom's Ghost--- What do you mean?

Orlando--- Your real name was Chona.

Mom's Ghost--- No, it was not. My "real" name, as you put it, was Oraida Piedra Negueruela. Piedra, from my father's side, Negueruela, my mother's.

Orlando--- So, why did everybody call you Chona?

Mom's Ghost--- That was my nickname, but you do not have permission to call me that.

Orlando--- I do not like that word. It means *chancho* or "pig."

Dad's Ghost--- Nicknames (*apodos*) are given by friends and others to someone they wish to mock. When derogatory, it feeds cruelty and diminishes the recipient. The solution is clear, and a remedy is readily available. Someone could say: Enough is enough! But they rather stay quiet, in order to blend in with others' cruelty. This posturing exemplifies a careless, pack like mentality while remaining inactive towards another's suffering.

Mom's Ghost--- Some people are cowardly and cruel. At birth, in Cuba, it was common for family and friends to adjudicate "funny names" to newborns. As children, all eleven of us were given nicknames: The boys--- Landín (Orlando), Tata (Onelio), Tito (Octavio), Papi (Obdulio), and Chirrino (Osvaldo). The girls were Chicha (Osilia), Avin (Olivia), Chona (Oraida), Ofelin (Ofelia) and Piojillo (Ondina), the youngest.

Dad's Ghost--- My friends also called me Gallego. That is why your friends called you likewise. After all, everyone says you are my *"imágen y semejanza"* (image and likeness).

Orlando--- My name was Orlando García Piedra at birth and still is today at seventy-four—except there is a hyphen now between my "two" last names. Of course, I dropped "de Jesus" as soon as I could. Why didn't you have the right to do likewise, Mom? You could have been Oraida Piedra Garcia. You did not have to "appear" to belong to anyone!

Mom's Ghost--- *Ay, Dios Mío!* (Oh, my God!) I did have the right; I just chose to use it socially.

Orlando--- *Tu nombre "registrado" es tan importante como tu palabra. Define quién eres.* (Your "registered" name is as important as your word. It defines who you are.)

Mom's Ghost--- You know very well who I am, or rather who I was. You are disrespecting me, and I beg you to stop this nonsense.

Orlando--- If you are intent on staying deaf to my authentic, well-meaning commentary regarding the very philosophical nature of our societal infrastructure, I will remain silent.

Mom's Ghost--- I think that is an excellent idea.

Orlando--- The Piedra family name appeared in the USA, the UK, and Canada between 1880 and 1920. My sister, Ana Maria, traced the name to a town in Cuenca, Spain, to the year 1601.

God--- What a census nightmare!

Chapter 5

In Utero, Birth, and Infancy

Orlando

In Utero

My first attachment experience equated to a primal need to remain close to my mother, my natural mentor, providing a sense of security and comfort. Our emotional bond solidified during her pregnancy, kickstarting the engine of subsequent social, emotional, and cognitive development.

Orlando--- I felt her warmth when she hosted me internally, and there is where I wanted to be.

Triggered by Mom's diet, the time of day, her level of activity, and maybe the amount of blood reaching me through her placenta, "intrauterine programming" (IP) controlled what was to become of me. Aware of my environment, interested in it, I developed feelings as it changed temperature, position, and chemistry; even before I took my first breath.

Orlando--- God, do you control IP?

God--- In science, the transition from nonliving to living entities---*evolution*---was not a single event, but a gradual process of increasing complexity. The passing on of traits from parents to their offspring induces the offspring cells or organisms to acquire the genetic information of their parents. That is how I created and built the universe. Environmental, genetic, and cultural factors affected your development from one stage to the next.

Orlando--- Is that how I became, both physically and psychologically, almost identical to Dad, more fair-skinned and a romantic dreamer, whereas Humberto favored the Piedra gene, darker (mulato) and hard-wired?

God--- Yes, remember, Orlando, my job was *Creation;* your job is *Evolution*. I also help with that. On the other hand, *genesis* speaks of beginnings---human beings made in My image, the climax of My creative activity, the heavens and the earth, light and darkness, seas and skies, land and vegetation, sun and moon and stars, sea and air and land animals, of marriage and family. Although imperfect, your superfamily was exceptional and amazing, one of my best human achievements. There is a lot more than a simple yes or no answer to the questions of where you come from and who you are, and how you survive. Have peace knowing I am always with you.

Mom's Ghost--- So, let us get started with your childhood memoir. Are you going to begin with your birth? Maybe I can help you with the details.

My Birth

I guess you already know this: I do not recall that day, August 24, 1946, the most amazing day of my life. Of the three major events that change a human's vital environment, and physical existence,---conception, birth, and death---the second one was probably the most exciting: certainly, the most amazing. I can only imagine my trip through the birth canal. Having delivered a few newborns, and observing the skull's shape, and the facial edema caused by severe trauma on cephalic presentations (head delivery,) I am glad that I do not remember that specific moment in time, but it must have been amazing.

Judging from what I know, it was my parents' happiest day, equal to the births of my brother Humberto thirteen months earlier, and my sister Ana Maria ten years later. I tell this story to you, joyous to have lived so long, thankful to have been so blessed, and lucky to have loved and been loved so deeply.

Mom--- His head was huge.

From listening to my mother's recollection of labor and delivery of her second son (me), I can only surmise, it was a struggle. This frequently dramatized complaint transferred a sense of guilt and bewilderment throughout my early childhood until I learned where babies come from and how they exit the mother's body. For her, a woman of faith, the experience was painfully physical but controlled by God from start to finish.

She often told her friends and family in casual conversation: *"Orlando nació con una cabezota que casi me rompe el cuerpo!"* (Orlando was born with a big head that almost broke my body!)

I was not born a twin, as my mother dreamed—she always reminded everyone of this unfulfilled wish. She once confessed to a friend that she had a dream where she saw Humberto and me graduating from college on the same day, dressed in matching cap and gown. Coming from an extended family, with ten siblings under the same roof, she may have had dreams of triplets/quadruplets/quintuplets, as many as possible, to feel the warmth and safety that came from her large family.

Infancy

During infancy and for a few more years, I remained dependent on Mom for most needs. Later, my childhood development was heavily influenced and guided by my brother, Humberto, thirteen months older and ten years wiser. This first attachment transfer shifted dependence from Mom to my older brother. I do not recall the moment in time when this occurred.

Orlando--- I am seeking memories from my earliest life moments in time to learn how I developed into Superboy, and who I am today. Learning how I viewed my world and acquired new skills helped me build coping mechanisms which changed me.

Mom's Ghost--- You were observing and understanding the world around you.

Dad's Ghost--- Your capacity to reason what was happening to you informed progressive reasoning stages, from fetus to birth into childhood and beyond.

God--- Environmental, genetic, and cultural factors affected you, inducing the speed of progress from one stage to the next.

Orlando--- I held my head up, rolled over, crawled, walked, and finally, ran---in that order---my first steps to becoming a superhero.

Any "abnormality" that could indicate developmental irregularities was immediately addressed. An attempt to correct it followed as quickly as possible in order to achieve "normality." Mother observed my progression toward the milestones of development to ensure that I was both physically and mentally developing normally. It is challenging now, to explain what I was going through, much less to analyze my feelings.

God--- That is why you are writing your book. Do not despair. First, figure out the journey from the beginning (1946 and 1947), then, early childhood, followed by middle childhood, your teens, and finally, adulthood. Your physical development followed a predictable sequence of events. Psychological development was unpredictable.

Part 2

The Cuba I Remember

[1948-1955]

Chapter 6
The Pre-Castro Era

Cuban history books written before the Castro era presented a narrative different from that written following the triumph of his Revolution. The United States' "revolutionary era" began with the American Revolution, pitting George Washington's army against Britain's. When "the people" spoke and fought for country, the revolutionary movement lead to America's Declaration of Independence, July 4, 1776.

Over a century later, in October 1868, Cuba's Declaration of Independence from Spain, was proclaimed in the Grito de Yara ("Cry of Yara"), by wealthy landowner Carlos Manuel de Céspedes. This signaled the beginning of the Ten Years' War, in which 200,000 lives were lost. Later, in 1895, led by Cuban nationalist and apostle José Martí, the Cuban War of Independence, again, pitted Cubans, who for years desired independence from Spain, against Spaniards.

On February 21, 1901, our constitution was approved.

Martí epitomized "the Cuban spirit" in his poem about truth and fear:

"In truth, man speaks too much of danger.
Poison sumac grows in a man's field,
the serpent hisses from its hidden den,
and the owl's eye shines in the belfry,
but the sun goes on lighting the sky,
and the truth continues marching the earth unscathed."

—JOSE MARTÍ

That state of mind, at liberty rather than in confinement or under physical restraint, translates a confident sense of personal power to determine immediate unopposed action without fear of consequential disaster.

Frankly, no one is completely free of anything, but the Cuban people, now citizens of a free country, exercised their right to pass on to their children their personal views. We had a constitution, on May 20, 1902, just as the US ratified its constitution June 25, 1788.

Constitutionalism—addresses ideas, institutions, rights, review, and limitations on governmental powers and serves to protect human rights. Through judicial review, fundamental rights are protected against legitimate authority and elected representatives of the people.

The Cuban constitution, prohibiting adult slavery, was advanced compared to the US. They both granted suffrage to non-landowning white males, and provided civil liberties, as opposed to subjection to an arbitrary or despotic government.

"That Cuba" was the country that received my paternal grandfather, Licinio Garcia Marcos, who migrated from Spain following World War I.

According to Fidel Castro, Cuba was not free until he freed it. This dissonance of the more recent Cuban history, as told by the Castro regime versus the one I know as fact, has not been written. My parents grew up in a free country! Much of the pre-Castro era was characterized by political violence. However, during the Castro regime, politics played no role. The Central Committee of the Communist Party ruled the country with an iron fist and changed its history without opposition.

This is not new. Over centuries, hundreds of countries dissolved, then re-built or disappeared. Fragmentation into different countries, and mass human displacements brought loss and pain; ends to lives previously lived.

Imagine there's no countries, it isn't hard to do, nothin' to kill or die for, and no religion, too… John Lennon and Yoko Ono wrote that in 1971. Is that possible?

It is, if the objective is life and not death; justice and not bias; freedom and not repression. Imagine life without freedom of speech, freedom of religion, and freedom of the press. Our Founders gave their lives to build a country with all those freedoms. In my country, Cuba, we did the same, but a totalitarian regime tricked the people into believing freedoms, previously "negated," would be guaranteed.

Philosophically, free-thinking and thinking without restraint facilitated parenting. However, education in one's civic duty must precede that for human rights. Like bootcamp, accountability and resilience must be present if Superman or God can help us efficiently. How sad when both governments, today's Cuba, and the US, feel compelled to protect children from parents to the degree we see today.

Imagine, today's parents and teachers, attempting to educate their children by sharing their deep-rooted philosophy that reflects their perspective on everything from education to history, society, religion, morals, and values dear to their heart. In Castro's Cuba, children at school are brainwashed daily, induced to believe there is freedom and liberty in Cuba.

"Imagine all the people livin' life in peace."
(JOHN LENNON, YOKO ONO)

* * * * *

The year 1933 marks many historians' views as the turning point in philosophical socioeconomic politics throughout the Western world. On January 30, Nazi leader Adolf Hitler was appointed chancellor of Germany by the German president, Paul von Hindenburg. The Nazis were coming!

The events in Europe, which followed the Great Depression and preceded World War II, had a profound impact on Cuban politics, and by extension on my parents' private lives and public environment. Worldwide, governments came and went, power changing sides as often as someone's first political mistake, or military coup d'état; one of the most unstable times in history, disturbing Cuba's social fabric.

On September 4, 1933, the "Sergeants' Revolt," also called the Cuban Revolution of 1933, was Sergeant Batista's first coup d'état. Lower-ranking officers and enlisted men successfully took over Cuba's Central Command Columbia barracks. It marked the beginning of Cuba's fight for "real" freedom, the fight against communism. Freedom was likewise demanded from fascism by oppressed people in Europe and Asia.

In 1934 the percentages of Cuban women working outside the home, attending school, and practicing birth control surpassed the corresponding percentages in nearly every other Latin American country. Women in Cuba had been elected to Cuba's House of Representatives and Senate, serving as mayors, judges, Cabinet members, municipal counselors, and members of the Cuban foreign service, all rights later guaranteed by the Constitution of 1940, which took effect on October 10. It was primarily influenced by the collectivist ideas that inspired the Cuban Revolution of 1933. Widely considered one of the most progressive constitutions at the time, it provided for land reform, public education, a minimum wage, and other social programs.

On March 10, 1952, Fulgencio Batista for the second time seized power on the island, proclaimed himself president and deposed the discredited president Carlos Prío Socarrás of the Partido Auténtico. Batista canceled the planned presidential elections and described his new system as a "disciplined democracy."

The evolution of the family from the traditional public realm that placed it wholly at the mercy of church teachings, now found itself thriving toward a more secular personal experience of private life. Before Castro, as I remember, Cubans were fun-loving people imbued with romanticism and folklore, sensuous music and erotic dance dominating nightclubs and private parties. But during the day, the country moved on hard work and professionalism and complex faith-based beliefs grounded in Christianity and African deities (Santería).

Street vendors stood on dozens of street corners throughout Havana and its suburbs. *Maniseros* selling *cucuruchos de maní* (hot peanut cones) loudly announced themselves with their typical *pregón*: *Si te quieres divertir, cómprame un cucuruchito de maní---Maní! El Manisero se vá. Caballero, no se vayan a dormir, sin comprarme un cucurucho de maní.* (If you want to have fun, buy me a peanut cone---Peanuts! The peanut vendor is leaving. Gentlemen, don't go to sleep without buying me a peanut cone.) Flavored slush of ice in paper cones (*granizados*), candy cones, orange juice, ice cream, and milk shakes, *croquetas* and *churros*, and peeled oranges, were also peddled curbside.

The Carnavales (Carnivals) in Havana were held for one month from mid-February to mid-March. Girls and boys dressed up in party costumes would ride with family and close friends sitting on the back of open convertibles and trucks parading next to large floats, similar to Mardi Gras (Fat Tuesday) in New Orleans, but more wholesome and family oriented. It was a family tradition, enjoyed fully by kids living in the major cities of Havana, Santiago de Cuba, Trinidad, Holguín, and Camaguey.

Blacks played their music and dances along with the *comparsas,* Carnival troupes and clubs organized by all races, including Chinese, Arabs, Jews, blacks, whites, and mulatto. Fifty years before, the massive participation of a population of African origin in the Cuban War of Independence resulted in a greater integration of the Afro-Cubans in social activities.

Dad's Ghost--- *Antes de la Revolución, nuestro país descansaba pacíficamente mientras dormíamos, sabiendo que nuestro trabajo* *diario ayudaba a aquéllos a quienes amábamos y creíamos con certeza que todos nos protejíamos unos a otros.* (Before the Revolution, our country rested peacefully as we slept, knowing our daily work helped those we loved and believed with certainty that all of us had each other's back.)

On New Year's Day 1959, Batista fled the island with an amassed personal fortune to the Dominican Republic, where strongman and previous military ally Rafael Leónidas Trujillo held power. My uncle Orlando Piedra was on that flight. A few days before, another uncle, Osvaldo (Chirrino) Piedra, copiloted Batista's family to New York City. Batista, denied entry to the US, eventually found political asylum in Oliveira Salazar's Portugal, where he first lived on the island of Madeira and then in Estoril, outside Lisbon.

Batista was involved in business activities in Spain and was staying in Guadalmina near Marbella on the Costa del Sol at the time of his death from a heart attack on August 6, 1973. He helped thousands, victims of the new order. He also helped my brother, Humberto, and me, financially get through medical school following Dad's death in Madrid, Spain, on May 21, 1967.

Chapter 7

The Garcias

Family Picture: <u>Standing</u>: Mauro and Dad. <u>Sitting</u> (left to right): Chely, me. Abuelo Tití (Licinio,) Abuela Esperanza, Humberto, and Mom.

Chalet Villa Zuli

<u>Standing</u>: Mom, and sisters, Olivia and Ofelia
<u>Sqwatting</u>: Dad

Abuelo Tití with Dad

November 6 and September 12, 1923 were the birthdates of my mother, Oraida Piedra Negueruela and my father, Humberto Garcia Pérez, respectively. Much of the populace's behavior during my parents' youth originated from world sociopolitical changes impacting the 1930s. As the dark cloud of WWII approached, 1933 crept upon them. Five years later, now in their teens, they were neighborhood friends in La Víbora, a suburb of Havana. Pictured at the gate of Villa Zuli, their faces radiate happiness and pleasure.

Early childhood begins at La Víbora (The Viper), the García's neighborhood.

Mom's Ghost---*Tu padre me seguía a todas partes.* (Your father followed me everywhere.)

Dad's Ghost--- *Con sólo mirarme, me volvía loco.* (By only looking at me, she would drive me crazy.)

Mom's Ghost--- *Yo quería cantar, pues tenía una voz muy clara y me sentía bien cantando, pero decidí casarme y hacer familia; nada me hubiera hecho más feliz que ser madre.* (I wanted to sing, for I possessed a noticeably clear voice and felt good singing, but I decided to get married and have a family; nothing would have made me happier than motherhood.)

Orlando--- But, Mother, you did sing. And with a beautiful voice, just like Doris Day!

La Víbora came with a warm Spanish Colonial Revival home, Villa Zuli, and a tamarind tree. Home to my paternal grandparents, Licinio and Esperanza, the Villa had been in the family for four generations. Esperanza's mother, my great-grandmother, Paula Liberata Calera Daniel, owned the house.

The Calera family owned several homes throughout the island, and they lived off the rents. My father and his sister, Tía Chely, lived at Villa Zuli when he and my mother met. Abuela Esperanza was a mild-mannered, thoughtful, loving person endowed with a keen sense of the source of others' intent. She lived with us throughout most of her life after becoming a widow. My favored human to be around.

Abuela Esperanza taught me the Cuban National Anthem at the piano and a game of cards called Brisca, a Spanish variant of the Italian card game Briscola or the equivalent to American poker.

She exampled self-restraint when confronted by anger, and was always judicious and prudent, qualities that allowed her to live her life in peace. Her one hundred percent commitment to the art of being a wonderful grandparent to go to, made her my favored granny.

In Spanish, with English translation, my best friend's dad, José Toraño, wrote a poem specifically for me to poke Grandma. The rhyme suffers in English, but it brought humor and laughter to family and friends, and especially to me.

"Cuando Abuela se enfermó"

Cuando Abuela se enfermó,
y el médico vino a casa
Yo le pregunté, ¿qué pasa?
Y él me dijo, se trancó!

¿Cómo, Cómo? dije yo,
y el doctor, muy asustado,
respondió:
Ésto es de cuidado,
pues tu abuela fué a Matanzas
y se rellenó la panza,
con diez libras de pescado.

Al oír ésto, dije yo:
Ampárala, Santa Adela
porque creo que mi abuela,
"El Manisero" cantó.

Mamá se descontroló
y Papá estaba asustado.
Pero ya todo ha pasado,
y hasta podemos cantar,
porque la hicieron cagar
con un tremendo lavado.

"When Grandma became ill"

When Grandma became ill
and the doctor came home
(to see her)
I asked him, What is wrong?
And he said: she shut down!

How, but How? I said
and the doctor, very frightened,
responded:
This is of concern, because
your grandma went to Matanza
And she stuffed her belly
with ten pounds of fish.

Hearing this, I said,
Bless her, Santa Adela
Because I think, my granny
Sang "The Manisero"
(The Peanut Vendor song)

Mom lost control
And Dad was scared
But all has passed
And we can even sing,
because "they" made her shit
with a tremendous enema.

My most vivid memory of Chalet Villa Zuli is the time I accidentally drove my tricycle into a rose bush located next to the steps leading up to the front door. It took forever to pry me away from the spinous shrubs climbing up the wall, trailing with stems armed with sharp prickles.

Esperanza--- *Mira, Chona, lo que ha hecho Orlando! Apúrate, está metido en el rosal! Niño, estás bien?* (Look, Chona, at what Orlando has done! He's gone into the rose bush! Son, are you OK?)

Esperanza's Ghost--- *Por poco me matas del susto!* (You almost scared the life out of me!)

I was a challenge.

Abuela Esperanza was home with me one day. Both Mom and Humberto had gone out somewhere. I was watching The Lone Ranger, a 1950s Western on TV, while violently manic, driven by the cowboy action on the screen, without fear, swinging back and forth on a rocking chair in the living room. Apparently, I swung back too far, fell off the rocker, and hit the back of my head on a glass tabletop behind me. The glass broke and cut my scalp. Profuse bleeding followed the injury. Granny was so upset, she became nervous, lost her composure, and began hitting me with her leather shoe, or *chancleta*, well known to *majadero* (misbehaved) Cuban kids as an instrument for corporal punishment.

After she calmed down, she took me to the bathroom and put pressure on the bleeding wound with a towel. After twenty or so stitches sown at the trauma ER to close the wound, we went back home with my head wrapped in a dressing.

Tia Chely married Mauro, a high-ranking official at the Treasury Department in pre-Castro Cuba, and, years later, a successful restaurant owner in Madrid, Spain.

Mom's Ghost--- They had two children, your cousins Mauro and Lula.

While living in La Víbora, my brother and I attended kindergarten. The class had approximately twenty students. We learned the colors, the numbers, and sang songs in class and outside, on the patio. Teaching was nurturing and supportive rather than competitive, as it helped us to grow emotionally, physically, and mentally in a then "recommended" way.

Humberto's Ghost--- We learned to read.

Mom would help us with each vowel and consonant. Typical questions before, during, and after reading helped us to understand what we read, initiating my knowledge of written vocabulary. Looking for words that related to things, people, and places I experienced while out and about probably encouraged me to incorporate my senses into clear phrases and sentences.

Humberto's Ghost--- We learned the Spanish alphabet in both capital and lowercase letters.
Mom's Ghost--- And in cursive, a style of penmanship used in most if not all schools.
Orlando--- What about English?
Mom's Ghost--- Basic English was compulsory. You and Humberto needed private classes at home to do better but our budget would not allow it. That kindergarten was a staple in our community. What you learned there was the foundation

that transferred later into your preschool, elementary and middle school.

The time of day was taught as a funny riddle. The teacher said: "When you give the time of day, if anyone asks about two minutes to two, how will you say it?" The class would scream: "TOTOTOO! Like a choochoo train. It was so much fun, I never forgot, and learned to tell time, in English, in one week.

Grandfather Licinio (Abuelo Tití) owned a small business, a men's sock factory called Star Knitting Mills and Dad helped him. Licinio was born in the town of Pedreñas, Santander---birthplace of the Spanish professional golfer Severiano "Sevi" Ballesteros, winner of the US Open Championship three times and The Masters twice. It was from this fishing village Licinio departed for Cuba, as so many other superheroes in their youth had done around WWI. He worked eighteen hours Monday through Saturday, taking six hours off on Sunday. When I woke up in the morning, he had already left for work, and when I went to bed at night, he was yet to get home.

One photograph of us together showing me in my grandfather's arms is the only visual I have ever needed. He was barely five feet tall, but his courage and determination were that of a ten-foot-tall giant. I believe Superboy inherited a large gene pool from him. I remember him with a clouded memory, but certain that he was pleasant, pleasurable, and enjoying of the loving we shared.

On Sundays, I was often in his arms as he carried me around the house or walked the neighborhood acting like a superhero. Listening to his stories as an immigrant from Spain, I began to learn how struggles make superheroes. Occasionally, he took us to downtown Havana to brag to his friends. He frequently visited my father-in-law-to-be Mr. Gómez's cafeteria, El Norma, located in Old Havana, holding my brother's hand in one of his and mine in his other. I was five years old. Eighteen years later, I married Gomez's younger daughter, María del Carmen, in San Juan, Puerto Rico.

Mom's Ghost--- *Así es como Virginia conoció a Licinio, mientras esperaba a su esposo, Gómez, a cerrar su negocio.* (That is how Virginia met Licinio, while sitting in the cafeteria waiting for Gómez to finish the day, clean up, and close the business.)

Virginia's Ghost--- *Breves ráfagas de emocionalidad explosiva sin más consecuencias que el miedo fugaz que afecta a otros que seguían preguntándose por qué estaba tan molesto, lo caracterizaron. Poco después de eso, se convertía en un hombre mayor de voz templada.* (Short bursts of explosive emotionality with no consequence other than the fleeting fear impinged on others who were kept wondering why he was so upset, characterized Licinio. Shortly after that, he would turn into a soft-spoken older man.)

Orlando--- This behavior was passed on to me, contributing to my unique emotional lability---a lifelong hindrance.

Mom's Ghost--- *Tu padre y tu tía Chely heredaron los genes de Esperanza en lo que respecta al comportamiento y la actitud ante la vida.* (Both your Dad and Aunt Chely, inherited Esperanza's positive atitude.) Her wisdom, but not her patience trickled down to the rest of you.

A vague recollection I have is that of a sunny day out in the back yard when Licinio killed a rabbit with one severe blow using the heel of his right hand to break the rabbit's neck.

Abuelo Tití (Licinio,) then peeled the skin off using a very sharp knife, slicing off any silver skin and sinew from the outside of the carcass, mostly on the outside of the saddle. Then, he cleaned it and cut it into pieces, the way you'd cut a chicken. I was both astonished and awed at his skill.

* * * * *

Baseball, as we played it during early childhood at la Víbora, was called *taco* (cork) or stickball. For a bat, we used a broomstick. For gloves, we used our hands. For a ball, we used anything round: a bottle cork wrapped with tape, or a tennis ball. My favorite was a handball, a hard rubber ball used in *pelota vasca* (jai-alai), a sport played in the Basque country of northern Spain. We wrapped *la pelota* with cloth tape for protection of all who caught the line drives, fly balls, and grounders.

We played las *cuatro esquinas* (four corners) using the four corners of the crossing of Gelaver and Josefina Streets *en mi barrio* (in my neighborhood). Each street corner was used as a base. We had to watch out for traffic.

My scariest recall involves fetching taco balls hit over the roof of a jail or clinic that housed mentally ill patients across the street from Villa Zuli. The balls landed in its unmanicured central courtyard patio, only accessed through an iron gate. Walled around the courtyard, eight or ten cells holding schizophrenics gesturing as they spoke---*"Ven Acá"* ("come closer")--- were enclosed by floor-to-ceiling vertical iron bars.

Their arms extended through the openings between the steel bars, sequentially flexing their index finger in a suggestive manner, which induced frequent nightmares of sadly unkept occupants of the darkened spaces inside the patio. Their hair was long, and the beards were large; knotted hair covering their lips, searching eyes appearing as they pushed the hair off their face to watch me. Scary!

One memorable day, Humberto and I left Villa Zuli and walked toward the railroad tracks separating two societies, one white, one black that lived so close and yet so far. We were wealthy; they were poor. We had the assets, they the liabilities.

However, they had fewer restrictions of movement and responsibilities than we had. Undoubtedly, we had a lot more options and access to wealth-creation opportunities than those on the other side of the tracks. It just seemed to me they had extraordinarily little, and we had a bunch, but both of us had superheroes. Although poor, they were not destitute---that is, suffering complete lack of the means necessary to meet basic personal needs such as food, clothing, and shelter. But they did not have baseball uniforms.

On another day, some kid from the other side came to our neighborhood and stole one of our gloves and a bicycle. I saw it happen and chose to not tell anyone.

Orlando--- *Mamá, por qué no nos dejas cruzar las vías del tren para ir a jugar con "los negros" que viven al otro lado?* (Mom, why don't you let us cross the railroad tracks to play with the negroes who live on the other side?)

Mom--- *Quédense de éste lado. No cruzen las vías.* (Stay on this side. Don't cross the tracks.)

It helped us understand the racial divide exampled by the Catholic Church at La Salle del Vedado school, then mimicked by our society. There were two Catholic schools, one for white (rich) students only, the other for (poor) black students in a segregated school system intended to distinguish and divide not just racially but also by socioeconomic status.

Only for the wealthy and upper-middle-class was there an excellent education available. The other, the school for blacks (la escuela de los negros, as we called it) educated the students with similar books, curriculum, and testing standards, but it was significantly tougher to make it to *La Universidad de la Habana* (Havana University) from that school. It had something to do with socioeconomic limitations and racism lingering still from centuries of abuse.

I remember the yellow school bus #2 picking us up at the corner of Gelaver and Josefina in La Víbora. As soon as we entered the bus, filled with white boys only, one of the students would start chanting, *"Margarito and Margarejo están aquí* ("they are here!") The cruel nicknames that mocked our appearance as twins, their laughter---"Ha, Ha, Ha,"--- and ridicule really upset us. We frequently got into fights; just one push or two and it was over, but the short burst of physicality gave us the peace of mind we needed to feel manly.

In the 1950s, the number of blacks becoming successful in business, medicine and engineering grew exponentially in Cuba, on a larger scale and at speed greater than other Latin American and Caribbean populations. Do not believe everything you hear from today's Cuban "historians" ruling the country: Cuba was not as backwardly illiterate and racist as they claim.

Orlando--- *Papá, por qué los negritos no tienen uniformes de pelota?* (Dad, why don't the little negroes have baseball uniforms?)

Dad--- *Pronto los tendrán* (They will soon have them); *os lo prometo* (I promise you.)

Dad crossed the railroad tracks with us. We joined the "colored" kids on their turf, de facto desegregating the neighborhood. After playing ball with those kids a few times, induced by their questions or their answers to my questions, I knew it was money that made us different; it allowed the purchase of those things I had, and they lacked.

Chapter 8

Stickball to Baseball

Me and Humberto in baseball uniforms

We wore blue-pinstriped-on-white uniforms with the Yankee "NYY" logo, or the Cuban professional baseball team Havana ("H" in red) Lions (Leones) or Almendares ("A" in blue) Scorpions (Alacranes) logo.

If my late brother authored my childhood memoir, he would begin this chapter by saying, *"Gallego, escúchame!"* ("Gallego, listen to me!"). He always demanded my immediate attention when he was about to say or do something. He had all the right to do so; after all, he was my big brother.

Baseball appeared in our childhood as early as 1950. Humberto and I participated in a children's baseball league played at the Tropical Brewery [La Tropical] Baseball Stadium in Havana. Three of my ten uncles played Class C professional baseball there, and they coached our team, the New York Yankees.

Orlando--- *Papá, cuándo empezaron a jugar los negros en las grandes ligas?* (When did black players join the majors?)

Humberto and I thrived on baseball history and statistical details.

Dad's Ghost--- *No sé exactamente. Jackie Robinson fué el primero.* (I do not know for sure. Jackie Robinson was the first.) I believe 1933 saw the birth of the Negro National League, and the first Major League Baseball All-Star Game was played at Comiskey Park in Chicago.

Humberto's Ghost--- I believe in 1945, the year I was born, Robinson led his team to victory in the International League World Series. Maybe it was 1946, Gallego, the year you were born. The next season, he moved up to the majors, becoming the first black man to play major league baseball.

Dad's Ghost--- *La integracion racial se llevó a cabo lentamente. En 1953, sólo seis de los dieciséis equipos de grandes ligas tenían un jugador negro en la lista.* (Racial integration proceeded slowly. By 1953, only six of the sixteen major league teams had a black player on the roster.)

We were always talking baseball.

Dad owned a family box in the baseball stadium at El Cerro, Havana, with six seats awfully close to home plate, so we could see every pitched ball moving up, down, and sideways as it approached the batter's box.

Orlando--- Who is that coming to bat?
Dad--- Sandy Amorós.
Humberto--- He never strikes out.

Orlando--- He always gets on base.

Dad--- Yes. That is because he is very quick to get to first base when he hits a ground ball. He also gets a lot of bases-on-balls because he is a short guy, more difficult for pitchers to throw strikes.

Humberto--- Does he play in the big leagues?

Dad--- Yes, he is going to play with the Brooklyn Dodgers.

Orlando---That's where Pee Wee Reese plays shortstop!

Dad---That is right.

Humberto--- They also have Sandy Koufax.

Dad--- Best pitcher in baseball.

Orlando--- What about Whitey Ford? He is a Yankee player. I bet you he is faster than Koufax!

Humberto--- No, Dad is right. The Dodgers are strong. They have Roy Campanella catching, and Duke Snyder in right field. Hard to beat.

Amorós's most memorable event in his baseball career, occurred in the sixth inning of the decisive Game 7 of the 1955 World Series. The Dodgers had never won a World Series and were now trying to hold a 2–0 lead against the New York Yankees. The left-handed Amorós came into the game at left field. The first two batters in the inning reached base. Yankees' catcher Yogi Berra, representing the winning run, came to the plate. Notorious for swinging at pitches outside the strike zone, Berra hit a left-curving opposite-field shot toward the left-field corner that looked to be a sure double, as the Brooklyn outfield had just shifted to the right.

Amorós, running at top speed, seemingly came out of nowhere, extended his gloved right hand, caught the ball, and skidded to a halt to avoid crashing into the fence near the 301-distance marker in the left-field corner of the famed Yankee Stadium. He then threw to the relay man, shortstop Pee Wee Reese, who in turn threw to first baseman Gil Hodges, doubling Gil McDougald off first. Hank Bauer grounded out to end the inning.

In today's flashy cable sports news television channel's "The Ten Top Plays," this one would be the Top Play of the Year, maybe the century.

Superboy--- I cannot wait for the *Serie Mundial* (World Series). I know the Yankees will win. We have the best team! Dad, do you think we can watch them play one day?

Dad--- *Un día iremos todos a Nueva York a ver un partido de la Serie Mundial, lo prometo.* (One day we will all go to New York to see a World Series game, I promise.)

Orlando--- WOW, Dad, you are the best!

Superboy --- Look, there is Camilo Pascual. Look at Pedro Ramos, and he is walking to the pitcher's mound.

Humberto --- Willie Miranda is up next. I bet you he will get a hit, probably a double.

Orlando --- I bet you he will hit a home run!

Professional players at El Cerro Stadium in Havana knew Dad. Sometimes, before the start of the game, as the players warmed up throwing the ball to each other, we would call to them, and once, the famous pitcher Camilo Pascual came to us and signed our gloves.

Orlando--- Look, Humbertico, I got my glove signed. Ask him to sign yours!

Pascual was already doing so as I was screaming my lungs out. We soon dominated the English baseball "lingo." Strike one, two, three *(uno, dos y tres)*; strike out *(está ponchado)*; ball one *(primera bola)*; one ball, two strikes *(una bola y dos strikes)*; a walk *(base por bola)*; bases loaded *(las bases llenas)*; line drive *(una línea)*; a single *(un hit o un sencillo)*. A pop fly *(un fly)* and you're out *(estás out)*. No runs, no hits, no errors *(sin carreras, hits ni errores)* and no runners left on base *(no dejaron corredores en base)*.

My favorite play was the "squeeze play," when there is a man on third and the batter bunts as the runner races to home plate. That, and stealing home were the two most exciting plays, but every pitch was awaited and enjoyed, every swing followed by one of us yelling, Wow!

Humberto was obsessed with baseball.

Humberto--- *Gallego, tírate de cabeza!* (Slide headfirst!)

He would scream in the middle of the night while sleeping. We slept in the same room, so I was startled and woke up thinking the house was on fire, or he was having an episode of acute appendicitis. As I looked to my right, I would find his silhouette on his bed; on his knees, moving his arms left and right or holding his thighs, he would yell again:

Humberto--- *Tira a segunda!* (Throw to second!)

Waking me up every time. I was not there when Mother delivered him, but I bet it was a left-handed-baseball-glove presentation the obstetrician saw as he came through the birth canal.

Orlando--- *Humberto, que coño te pasa!* (What the hell is wrong with you!) I would scream. *Duérmete y cállate la singada boca. Te voy a dar un piñazo!* (Go to sleep and shut the fuck up. I am going to smack you!)

It was all about stickball and baseball

Chapter 9
The Piedras

Rita and José / Rita and her children / Rita and her grandchildren

Rita Negueruela "de" Piedra delivered eleven children and gave them all names starting with the letter O. Thus, the girls (with their nicknames): **O**silia (Chicha), **O**livia (Avin), **O**raida (Chona – my mother), **O**felia (Ofelin), and **O**ndina (Piojillo); and the boys: **O**nelio (Tata), **O**rlando (Landin), **O**scar, **O**ctavio (Tito), **O**bdulio (Papi), and **O**svaldo (Chirrino).

A friendship conceived as a team effort constantly mimicked the love among, her and her progeny, the stronger picking up the weaker. Life in the Piedra household depicted a hand-me-down philosophy, whereby the younger inherited clothing, toys, and academic supplies. Six boys and five girls can make a lot of noise, and they did. Rita's mother, Lola, lived with them, as well as an aunt, Margarita, and two uncles, Obdulio (Yuyo) and Antonio (Cotingo), both in frequent need of psychiatric care.

Mi Abuela (Grandma) *Rita* cooked for seventeen people every day, washed and ironed clothing worn by her husband and children, and was committed to them through common interests and daily needs. On one hand, they felt an all-for-one and one-for-all closeness; on the other, they could not wait to leave the home and become independent. These behaviors were noticed and jotted down by both Humberto and me. We saw our path through theirs.

It was Rita's creation or learned philosophy that energized their home. My continued growth to Superboy began to solidify as I developed amongst them. Neither the men nor the women accepted physical or psychological defeat, in line with their mother's parenting philosophy. Their attitude exampled individuals who did not take shit from anybody.

People in the initial stages of a romantic relationship, as well as during pregnancy, offer unconditional Storge (familial love), as the family is built from the ground up; but they find only the need and dependency of Eros, as most women feel nature's gift inside them. Rita owned this feeling eleven times.

Rita and José raised their eleven children in a farming community, Arroyo Naranjo, where the couple moved the family in the late 1930s. Natural water described its fluvial geology. Blessed with a small creek that washes a stream bed that temporarily fills and flows after enough rain, the farm was close to two small provincial towns, Güira de Melena and San Antonio de los Baños, the former, birthplace to her first five, the latter, to her last six, both in Havana Province.

We spent a lot of time at *La Finca* (the farm) with cousins, uncles, and aunts. Abuelo (Abo) José, a policeman who came home from work every day to find a clean house but rarely a quiet home, owned the property. Flash floods are common in *arroyos* following thunderstorms. In Cuba, any small river might be called an arroyo, even if it flows continually and is never dry.

I believe this place is where my lifelong environmental allergies began. The area was known for *naranjales,* fields of orange groves, its perfume as sweet as the fragrance of citrus blossoms. That smell remained in my memory when years later I lived in central Florida, full of beautiful citrus groves spread through a hilly country bursting with oranges, grapefruits, lemons, limes, and tangerines.

THE PIEDRA MEN

Coronel **Orlando** (Landín) Eleno Piedra

Former Cuban Secret Police and FBI chief, married Maria Antonia (Cuca) Brito, daughter of Colonel Antonio Brito, the chief of the National Police Force from 1940 to 1944. They had two sons, Amaury (Pepe) and Esteban (Estebita), who was adopted. I did not see Landín often. When I did, he was always smiling, portraying a sedate attitude indicative of peace and safety. I never saw or heard him worried, concerned about our safety; he was obviously considering his men's ability to guarantee the country's welfare. He took several bullets during his service for the nation. I dreamed to do the same as I grew up; to own his amazing power so I could become Superboy.

I went to the Bureau Building once. Landín gave me a tour. In the basement, the FBI underground target practice range was where I first held a gun in my hand and fired it without anyone's help. I was eleven years old. I am certain I carry his name, Orlando, as Mother's prayers to her angels, the Virgin Mary, and God, sent petitions and wishes for his safety in exchange for her promise to always behave as a good Christian. There was nothing more important to Uncle Landín than family and country.

Following political exile, he chaired the Anti-Communist Foreign Legion of the Caribbean *(Legión Extranjera Anticomunista del Caribe),* an anti-Castroist right wing paramilitary group based in Dominican Republic. As a continuation of his lifelong fight against communism, in 1959, a few months following our family's forced departure from Cuba, Orlando and his group, in part funded by the CIA, staged a failed attempt to overthrow Castro.

Uncle Orlando died in Hialeah, a city in Dade County (home to Miami) on July 12, 1999, at the age of eighty-two. Like President Batista, Landín was a Mason.

Congressman **Onelio** (Tata) Eleno Piedra

Born in 1916, married Dalia Torres. They had two children, José Agustín and Onelito. In Cuba, Uncle Onelio was well known for his huge smile and friendly character, which allowed him to win a congressional seat in Cuba's Senate.

A large, lit Partagás cigar was always in his mouth, transferred to his hand only when speaking. I loved his joyous personality and work ethic, appearing playful while running national business.

Following the triumph of the Revolution, Tata moved to Guaynabo, Puerto Rico, and worked with his brother-in-law, Gustavo Rey, for several years until his death from a ruptured abdominal aortic aneurysm while waiting for surgery at University Hospital-San Juan, located in Rio Piedras, San Juan, Puerto Rico.

National Police Guard **Oscar** Eleno Piedra

A member of the president's personal mounted motorcycle guard, married Leonor Miguel; they had one daughter, Lizette. Oscar told me once, nearing the end of his life, "Bring your father to Miami so he can stay with Chonita (Mom) forever; that was her wish." I told him I would.

Dad had passed a few years earlier. Interred in a cemetery in Madrid, Spain, where he died, Dad was buried "sandwiched" between Mauro Folgosa's and his father's bones; Mauro owned a grave that allowed three corpses. My sister, Ana Maria, my wife, Mary Carmen, and I brought Dad's ashes back to the US at Oscar's bidding.

One day, in Miramar, Cuba, I was home, midmorning on the weekend, when I heard the roaring sound of motorcycle engines getting louder by the second. I knew it was Oscar and his buddy, Oscar Brito, Cuca Brito's brother, approaching my house riding black-and-white Harley-Davidsons. I ran outside to meet them. I was a short nine-year-old.

My heart was pounding from adrenaline flowing through it. Suddenly, I stopped and stood in front of them, awed by everything I saw and heard. They did not turn off the engines, knowing full well the excitement I felt as I stood still, looking up at them in uniform. Huge black leather boots, tight below the knees, widened above them to surround folds of beige khaki pants that stopped at the waist held in place by a wide navy-blue belt with a large shiny gold buckle.

I dreamed of that moment for days, asking Mom to please buy me one. I got my Zundapp motorcycle two years later.

Professional baseball player **Octavio** (Tito) Eleno Piedra

Married Juanita and had a son, Titico. Tito was the best baseball player in the family, and one of the best in the country. Dad often took us to see him play at the Tropical Brewery Baseball Stadium.

In 1959, like the rest of the family, he was forced to leave Cuba. A baseball fan throughout his life, Tito watched every major league game he could while living in exile in Miami.

Of the six Piedra brothers, he was the last one to die. I often visited him at his Miami home, especially during Christmas, when he roasted a whole pig in his backyard deliciously prepped all night with cloves, garlic, salt, black peppercorns, sour orange juice, lemons, onion, oregano, and olive oil. It cooked for five hours in a large roaster called *caja china*. With a super crunchy bacon-like skin and super-tender juicy meat, it was an amazing meal for the family and friends attending the event.

Obdulio (Papi) Eleno Piedra

Married Gladys Camps; had a son, Obdulio (Duly) and two daughters, Marilu and Liliana (Bebita). In Cuba, he worked for Public Works. The kindest man I have ever known, there was nothing anyone could hold him from giving away "the shirt on his back."

In Cuba, he was often present at Rita's home, extremely family-oriented, helping out with all things going wrong; broken appliances, leaking roofs, electrical cables needing repair, kitchen and bathroom re-dos, and painting. He built an extra room in the back of his home in Miami to house immigrant relatives and helped us in ours with the yard. I am still close to his children.

The epitome of kindness, the one "outlier" who lived under the radar within the comfort and peace that comes from non-confrontation and tempered ambition. Humility was his biggest asset, simplicity his moto, unconditional family support his purpose, and generosity his mission. A great guy to emulate.

Papi was adored in the family, but he had a special place in mom's heart. I recall dozens of times hearing her talk about her brother as if she were describing a saint. There was a special relationship between them shared in public. *"Papi viene hoy a arreglar el jardín"* (Papi is coming today to work on the garden.) *"Voy a cocinar algo especial para el"* (I will cook something special for him.) It was like a mother-son relationship.

Fighter pilot, Cuban patriot KIA 2506 Brigade, Bay of Pigs, Lieutenant **Osvaldo** (Chirrino) Eleno Piedra

The youngest of the Piedra men, married Vivian Diaz. Chirrino was and will always be our family and national hero.

He fought Castro's guerrillas in Cuba's highest mountains, la Sierra Maestra. I deeply cherish the memory of the time he took me to the Air Force Command Airfield. He helped me climb up the wing and into the rear seat of a two-seater fighter jet parked in formation next to a dozen or so precisely spaced-in-parallel aircraft. For months, I dreamed of Superboy starting the engine and taking off into the sky.

Later, he flew over Ciénaga de Zapata during the Bay of Pigs invasion, where his plane was shot down by American-built aircraft while supporting the beach landing. The bravest member of our family, he left us while still young at the age of twenty-three. A recording of his last minutes made by another fighter jet with open radio near him was shared with our family at Rita's home in Miami.

Recently, I met a man who participated in the invasion who knew Chirrino well. The man told me, at a lunch for La Salle alumni, he was present as deacon in the aircraft that recorded the aforementioned conversation between Chirri and the pilot who shot him down. That man gave Chirri his last rites over radio seconds after his airplane was hit by gunfire. Chirrino's name, Osvaldo Piedra Negueruela, is in scripted in bronze at the Cuban Memorial Bay of Pigs monument, located at Southwest 13th Avenue, between 8th and 12th street in Miami's "Little Havana."

THE PIEDRA WOMEN

Osilia (Chicha) Elena Piedra

Married Gustavo Rey, a respected business owner, and together they had two sons, Humberto, and Gustavo. President Batista was the best man at their wedding. The oldest Piedra, Chicha was also the kindest, funniest, most jovial, loving, and tolerant, welcoming everyone who visited her home in Guaynabo, Puerto Rico.

Among many anecdotes, number one has to do with a painting she asked me to buy and bring her from Spain. During my medical school years, I became assistant tour guide at the famous Prado Museum. The painting she requested, Murillo's *Ascención de la Virgen,* was commissioned and stunningly reproduced, at exactly the size ordered, for me by a Prado resident painter, and I carried it to San Juan by air during a Christmas holiday. Measuring 2 by 1 meters (approximately 80 by 40 inches), it was a feat to bring it on the airplane, but a bigger concern was where to hang it in the house.

Upon arriving at Osilia's home, it became obvious the Catholic work of art would not fit any wall except one in the foyer. In order to show her and Uncle Gustavo Rey, *La Ascención*, we had to move the dining room table out into the living room, lay the painting on the dining room floor, and open it. Then, Gustavo came down the stairs, having no clue of what, where, from whom, how big or expensive; it was always an extravagant surprise. *Dicho sea de paso* (it goes without saying), Gustavo's jaw dropped in disbelief, exclaiming: *"Chicha, estas loca?"* (Chicha, are you crazy?) The painting remained in their home for years for her, her family, and all their friends to admire and pray.

Olivia (Avín) Elena Piedra

Married David (Quico) Almeyda, a physician: they had two sons, Alejandro and David José, and a daughter, Sylvia. A devout Catholic, Avín left Cuba in 1956 for Georgia, where Quico trained as an anesthesiologist. She then moved to Houston, Texas, to raise her children.

Her life was tough, away from her family whom she missed dearly, with a husband who worked day and night at the medical center. Her first child and granddaughter died young, as well as Quico, run over by an oncoming car he did not see coming.

Avín always had her home opened to all family members who, in one way or the other: health or financial distress, needed help. My mother and my sister stayed at their home for almost four years following Dad's death.

Oraida (Chona) Elena Piedra

My mother, married Humberto (Dad) and had two sons, Humberto, and me, and one daughter, Ana Maria. There was no better mother on the globe than Mom. She embodied the deepest love any human being could offer. Characterized by a combination of feelings, behaviors, and sacrifices shared while raising me and my siblings, her unconditional love protected us day and night, whether together or separated by oceans and mountains. Leaving her personal needs behind, Mother was always present in our hearts and minds.

I was blessed to have her in my life, lucky to be present at her side the day she passed, enchanted by her inner beauty, encouraged by her character, educated by her knowledge, grown by her wisdom, and at peace knowing her immense love was mine forever. I am uncertain as to what exactly will happen when my time comes. I do know that she will flood my path with sunshine as I seek her through the clouds. Finally, expectant to reach her soul and again celebrate another life with her, together again, we will have a new beginning, a blessed opportunity to enjoy a better life, for which I am forever grateful.

Ofelia (Ofelin) Elena Piedra

Married Salvador Pérez and had a son, Salvador (Chachi), and a daughter, Mayra (Mayrita), variously *"La Flaca" or "La Zurdita"* (the Thin One or Lefty). Ofelia was jovial and wholesome, somewhat naïve, and she loved arts and crafts. An assistant nurse at one time, she was long associated with health care, but unfortunately, mostly as a patient.

Disabled from a malignant bladder tumor for many years, Ofelín was always talking about the family: "My brother or sister---*nickname*--- is the best looking, most intelligent, caring, loving, or amazing..." at any positive superlative imaginable. She died young from bladder cancer on September 8, 1981.

Ondina Elena Piedra (Piojillo)

Married Orlando Fidalgo, the architect who built our house at El Biltmore, Cuba, and then, Abuela Rita's house in Coral Gables, Florida. They had a son, Eduardo, and a daughter, Rita María (Chanti). Ondina was a ball of fire.

Beautiful and sexy, she was both smart and very well educated, with a degree in pharmacy from the University of Havana and a degree in social work and psychology from the University of Florida in Gainesville.

She worked at Jackson Memorial Hospital in Miami as a pharmacist and later at Miami Senior High School as a counselor, becoming my mother's best friend and my second favored aunt (after Chely).

With such a large family, my mother grew up in a house where there was no isolation possible for bathing, using the bathroom, dressing, and undressing; a request to "turn around" or look the other way was issued frequently, as a saving grace to modesty. There was no social agreement among them, but rather a group conquest of space.

No one slept alone; beds had to be shared, excellent for *shyness* training. It was difficult to keep personal objects from others or hide feelings of discomfort affecting anyone in the house.

Rita's Ghost--- *El espacio era limitado, por lo que todas las necesidades de carácter fisiológico o emocional se llevaban a cabo en presencia de otro.* (Space was limited, so all physiological or emotional needs were carried out in the presence of another.) The girls could not menstruate without everyone knowing it; the calendar shared the same wall space in the kitchen as the school schedule, baseball practice drills, and the grocery list.

Mom's Ghost--- It all became a frequent source of stress in the lives of those less tolerant in the household, especially the elderly, the siblings, and other close relatives sharing the home.

Rita was the orchestra leader, the "maestra" (leader) of ceremonies.

José's Ghost--- We were not politicians, who seek support from the people through rhetoric delivered with empty promises and pretenses while wearing fancy clothing and enticing smiles. We moved in the opposite direction, driven by unwavering commitment to Christian teaching and patriotism.

Mom's Ghost--- *Mi familia estaba muy unida, con muchos pliegues y arrugas entrelazados por la sangre, el sudor, las risas y las lágrimas.* (My family was as tight knit as they come, with lots of folds and wrinkles interlocked by blood, sweat, laughter, and tears.)

Rita's Ghost ---*Yo no sé cómo ustedes manejaron a ésos muchachos,* (I do not know how you handled those boys)— referring to my brother and me—*pero Chonita, pensé que ibas a* *tener que buscar un regimiento de infantería para protejerlos* (but Chonita, I always thought you would have to find an infantry regiment to protect them).

I was Rita's third grandson, born into the Piedra family, after Pepe (Landin's son) and my brother Humberto. My six uncles and five aunts in their late twenties---the oldest, Osilia; the youngest, Osvaldo still a child---lived in a country known for progressive thinking, a bastion of gender equality and women's rights. It was challenging for us to follow our ancestor's path, as it was for them to follow ours. We were wild, interested only in emulating Dad and the Piedra men.

The men were not particularly well educated; none of them held a college degree. While they were young, they worked menial jobs, like trolly driver, bus ticket collector, machine operator, and police trainee in the Police Academy. I needed an invisible and inaudible imaginary friend to join them while at work in their collective efforts, help them "save the world," reach the ordered society that would allow everyone to prosper, a superhero.

Superboy would be right in there with them, leading the investigation of criminals (Landín) in my *perseguidora* (police car), protecting the president on my motorcycle (Oscar), fighting guerrillas in the mountains (Chirri) in my fighter jet, hitting home runs out of the ballpark (Tito), winning a congressional seat (Tata), or admiring (Papi) kindness.

It came naturally to be extremely competitive. I know for certain that Superboy learned this behavior from the Piedras.

God--- Everyone knows Piedra means "stone."

Part 3

Adapting to Expectations

(1956-1958)

Chapter 10

New Realities

Middle childhood begins around age six, approximating primary school age. It ends around puberty (age twelve or thirteen), which typically marks the beginning of adolescence. At that point in my life, we were wealthy, considered a "well-to-do" family, well-connected, upward moving; some uncles and aunts working-middle-class, all civil, patriotic, courageous, and financially healthy. Obviously, they also had a myriad of problems, financial, as well as personal.

Already at La Salle del Vedado school, where I attended first through sixth grade, I came home each day tired after a long day in school, but Mom always found a way to "convince" us to do our homework. I was still learning how to relate to those around me in a way I could understand. Things I thought were real during social interactions, for example, often turned out untrue. I began to realize not all was going to be my way or the highway, I just did not know why.

As I write this, I wonder, what did I do during those years in limbo to get what I wanted? What tricks did I use to get others to believe I was worthy of their attention and compassion? Which motivation and psychological interaction with my environment and those who crossed my path was key to influencing my characteristic way of thinking, feeling, and behaving?

thinking---finding an answer to a question or the solution to a practical problem, *feeling*---being sensitive or intuitive toward understanding my world, and

behaving---meeting standards of what is proper or decorous?

Over time, my identity would become fragmented, while enriched, by moving at a young age from one country to another. I did not feel "Cuban" when, at ten and eleven years old, we traveled to Indiana to attend Culver Military Academy, or to Palm Beach, Florida, for Graham-Eckes School, nor at twelve years of age, when my family came to the US "for good." Nor at seventeen, when we moved to Spain following my graduation from Miami Beach Senior High School in the summer of 1963. I always adapted, aware of my "duty" to meet expectations surpassing others around me.

In 1953 we moved from La Víbora to Miramar, our home until 1957.

Orlando--- Mom! I'm done with homework!

Not true, just wanted out of the house, into the neighborhood street to play.

Mom--- You need to do your homework!

Silence. I was gone before she finished the sentence, heading out for a ride on my Zundapp, or to find Pepe to play, or to go to Miramar Yacht Club.

These were exciting years, as I experienced a period of rapid maturation and social growth. I gained the physical coordination to dress well, even tie a knot in a tie, and complete tasks that allowed me to function independently from my parents and away from the safety of my home environment. The certainty of being safe from harm if at arm's length to Humberto guaranteed peace of mind.

In 1956, I was supposed to begin school abroad by seeking to become more independent, but instead rejected tasks and chores that could lead to a more responsible lifestyle. I was ten years old. The choice to dismiss responsibilities that stole precious playtime from a short after-school day equated to my preference for no accountability. My attachment to Humberto had occurred around age six. His influence on anything and everything I did, thought, or felt was strongest through my middle childhood and teen years.

Humberto --- *Gallego, ven aca!* (Gallego, come here.)

That is how my brother called me, *"Gallego,"* a nickname shared with our father, Gallego only to his close friends. These are the first words I recall coming out of my brother's mouth. The word *Gallego* was used as a colloquial masculine noun from Spain by way of Latin America. Example usage in a sentence best explains the reasoning behind intent: *Yo creo que el dueño de la tienda de la esquina es Gallego* (I think the owner of the corner store is *Spanish*). If Gallego is a man from Galicia, and Galicia is only one region in Spain, among many others, why would this word define all Spaniards? The reason is that most Spanish immigrants to Cuba were from Galicia, Spain; they were "Gallegos."

Humberto--- *Ven ahora, que te necesito.* (Come now, I need you.)

My relationship with Humberto brought real or fictitious meaning to specific interpretations of events that filled our often-silly childhood. Competition was fierce. I assume the motives were primarily jealousy and anger—both reflecting resentments lasered at each other as similar-age rivals competing in every imaginable way; typical brothers, enjoying or suffering each other's success and advantage, or sadly each other's failures. Humberto and I were awfully close. I was only thirteen months younger and loved teasing him—and he enjoyed it also.

Humberto--- *Gallego, estás hablando basura.* (You are talking trash.)

Orlando--- *Véte para el carajo.* (Go to hell.)

Carajo literarily means the lookout basket in the topmast of a Spanish galleon ship. Sailors would get very seasick when assigned to this post. So, when they thought of mutiny, the captain would send them up to the *carajo* as punishment. It was truly a living hell.

Humberto's Ghost--- *Coño, no me jodas.* (C'mon, stop bothering me).

Coño is a way to emphasize or stress a wide variety of emotions, to focus attention or highlight something we want to say. "*Ñoooó, que barato!*" ("Damn, this is cheap!") Or you can use it like "*Cóño, págame lo que me débes!*" ("Look, pay me what you owe me!") Or "*Coñó, me robaron la bicicleta!*" ("Shit, someone stole my bicycle!")

Humberto and I, as well as most of our friends and the Cuban population at large, used the word frequently, almost in every other sentence to stress emotions.

As a child, Humberto was considered a high achiever, appearing to excel at different endeavors. In math, for example, he would add, multiply, and divide large numbers by thinking it through, without paper and pencil. I, on the other hand, was not interested in sharing knowledge, instead holding it secret so no one really knew how intelligent or stupid I was. Thus, I was treated as an average kid, insecure and immature, a dreamer demanding little attention, not asking many questions, whereas Humberto appeared to have answers for everything.

Like most people, our private life was influenced by multiple factors, primarily faith, hope, dreams, realities, financial status, and parental guidance; but mostly by peer pressure, and the fear of getting caught doing something prohibited.

"Little people" often experience alarm and dread followed by agitation as they process adults' demands for "mature" behavior. At this age, much of what we did or didn't do hinged on whether we thought it would lead to trouble, versus earning love and approval for successfully meeting parental expectations. In our case, it all happened surrounded by true love from common people in upscale neighborhoods and school.

Such beautiful surroundings and frequent playful activities manufactured a perfect childhood experience. Unbeknownst to me, we were the envy of many children who lacked a clean environment, expensive cars, and a blessed lifestyle, with plentiful food, servants, the newest of everything, good health, and a solid education.

We started to enjoy teamwork, mostly through participation in team sports. My two best friends, René, and Pepe were always around. Many life moments came directly into my awareness, while just as many filtered through Humberto.

Dad was absent for the most part, but Mother frequently reminded us of our duty to hold ourselves accountable for our actions and lead by example. She would hammer basic "rules of the road." Every weakness hunted me, but sloth was the worst. As a dreamer, as opposed to Humberto, who epitomized a doer attitude, I lost precious time going from one useless fantasy to another. During those days preceding our first trip abroad to attend school, we received plenty of tough love. That is precisely what I miss most.

God--- Orlando, you must figure out whether your lack of positive feeling was a cause or effect of your frequent isolation from others and your lack of faith in me.

Humberto's Ghost--- Yeah. You made it exceedingly difficult for me to pull you out of doldrums.

Orlando--- Depression is a horrible feeling that invades every thought and keeps you stuck.

I often felt alone when Mom was not around.

Mom's Ghost--- So, your responsibility to feel whole through your own efforts was weakened?

Orlando--- Yes! We were not eleven siblings supporting each other.

Mom's Ghost--- I see. Your resolve was lacking because you were only two. Please, give me a break. If you try hard to reach the best you can be, less time will be spent trying to convince me you can't.

Dad's Ghost--- She never asked either of you to be perfect.

Mom's Ghost--- Listen, my expectations of how far each of you would go and how quickly you would get there had a lot more to do with your personal commitment to hard work than to any pressure I could apply.

With political tensions rising, my parents wanted me and Humberto out of the country, so a search for a foreign school began in earnest. But first, they figured we must learn English. Our English teacher, Miriam Ledo, came highly recommended by Cuba's first lady, Marta Fernández Miranda *de* Batista.

It was winter in Havana, January 1956. A third attempt on Uncle Landín's life, carried out two weeks earlier during Christmas, had failed. As his family ran for cover, the pass-by machine-gun shooting of his home on 5ta Avenida, Miramar's main boulevard, blew out all the glass windows in front of the house. Two of his personal military escort assigned to guard his home were killed. The shattered windows exploded, injuring those sitting in the living room. My Aunt Cuca, Landín's wife, and guests sustained superficial cuts and bruises as they ducked for cover. Superboy was too young to help.

Fifteen years earlier, Cuca's father, Comandante Brito, the nation's chief of police in the late 1930s around Batista's first term as president of the Republic of Cuba, was assassinated in Havana while filling up his gas tank.

Things were about to get worse. Within the next two years, 1957 and 1958, several members of General Fulgencio Batista's government would die gunned down by members of Fidel Castro's 26th of July Movement (MR-26-7). Those who felt threatened by violence began searching for ways to protect their families from harm. Superboy was eleven years young.

Miriam Ledo--- Practice asking questions to learn the meaning of the words in a sentence, things you will need to know in the American school.

Miss Ledo was a tough cookie. Only twenty-five, her youthful energy transmitted a take-no-prisoners attitude, which drove a clear message: "Don't fuck with me." I tried to learn as many words as I could memorize. The first words we learned were curse words I would never share with her. Mother gave us three months to get up and running with our English. There was no time to waste. Miss Ledo was obsessive-compulsive about doing her job right. She demanded plenty from us while exploring our capacity to be reasonable and rational, owning sound judgment. Mother, meanwhile, was looking hard abroad for the best school money could buy.

Miriam Ledo--- Going forward, your interests must be triggered by the wish to communicate with American kids. Both of you will approach several children who will want to play with you; be vigilant of their intent, and trust what you learned here.

I loved watching American TV. I was hyperactive, so a fan of the fifties television program *Dennis the Menace,* about an energetic, trouble-prone, mischievous but well-meaning kid.

Dennis often tangled with anyone close enough to victimize. Basically, a good, well-intentioned boy, he always tried to help people but most often wound-up making situations worse.

The show was one of my favorites, as I very much identified with the fictional Dennis. Both Mom and Dad, as well as extended family, would brag among themselves and to their friends with pride and a *sense* of *fulfillment,* boasting at the "macho" and wild behavior we exhibited. Many onlookers were terrified, left wondering about parental competence and apparently lax school guidelines for imposing some discipline to our rearing. My parents viewed this behavior as acceptable conduct intended to strengthen self-image and male performance, very desirable for character building. Others were left clueless and scared.

Mom and Dad encouraged Humberto and me to be wild and crazy. Meanwhile, Ana Maria's education was structured for a lady meant to fulfill a complex system of beliefs, mores, and customs held by Cuban society. Family social gatherings during the pre-Depression era demanded strength and resolve, as well as morally sound adult behavior in public, especially in the presence of children. But men could get away with anything.

Mom's Ghost--- I always prayed for both of you and then Ana Maria. Most of your dad's life was an example of solid ethical and moral values, except fidelity.
Orlando--- What do you mean?
Mom's Ghost--- Do not worry. Just remember that *lust* may lead to a *false pride,* misguided behavior that will always get you in trouble.
God--- Be careful, Chona. Without forgiveness, you cannot stay in Heaven.

Mom was right in fearing Dad's social behavior may transfer the wrong message to her children. El Floridita was his favored meeting place, a watering hole my dad frequented as a member of the "boys club" of Havana. It was patronized by young and middle-aged businessmen holding the reins of power in a city known for its buoyant night life and thrill-seeking lifestyle. Hemingway was a regular customer.

Dad was no different from most Cuban males, a victim to the first sin, *lust*. Accepted by some women and encouraged by most men in social environments at the time, having a girlfriend or "*querida*" meant the man was more "*macho*" and wealthier, and the wife more "understanding." It transferred a confusing message of uncertainty. To our detriment, and that of our closest friends' families and relatives, it was okay for us all—society at large—to behave that way, even if it resulted in a broken home. Although my parents kept all this well hidden from us, I am now convinced, looking back with wisdom's eagle eyes, that we children picked up behaviors and subtle confrontations exampled by both young adults and those adults who raised us.

Humberto, Ana Maria and Me

Mom, me, and Abuela Esperanza

Chapter 11

New Challenges (Adolescence)

Humberto and I studied abroad for a couple of years while in middle school—two summer camps at Culver, Indiana, and boarding school at Palm Beach, Florida. Each time, leaving Cuba for the United States, we changed place, nationality, language, the legal system, philosophical identity, and historical relevance, mostly unprepared to face new realities, meet new challenges, and conform at such a fast pace. Adapting quickly was a challenge.

Nevertheless, our Christian values and education were similar to those of the families we met: Remain loyal to family and friends, have faith in God, practice what you preach, value true friendships, seek commitment and responsibility, always choose the right over the convenient, and have hope, rather than fear.

Consciously reasoning my present was key to acknowledging my past, and vice versa. But I was immature. My most formidable barrier was ADHD. Attention-deficit/hyperactivity disorder is a neurobehavioral disease characterized by a combination of inattention, hyperactivity, and impulsive behavior. I had great difficulty sitting still, problems maintaining attention on school or homework, and frequently responded before thinking. I was fidgety, restless, and talked without pause. My rebellious personality colored by ADHD began to show.

My Cuban Catholic culture was built on a network of artificial instincts and religious norms (dogma) that enabled millions of strangers—the Cuban population at large— and my parents to cooperate in a common mission to support child development throughout the island. This "progress" in social awareness brings every child from less cognit stages (early childhood) to more mature behavior---a continuum through adolescence to adulthood. I remember extraordinarily little from those early playtime experiences with friends and not-so-friendly kids but assume my view of the world followed in parallel with theirs.

Critical questions regarding the veracity or falsity of my *conscious reasoning*---what I thought was true---and *wisdom*---what I learned from experience (mostly painful ones) as a consequence of lifestyle choices remained unanswered as I moved toward creating Superboy, the kid, and then, Superman, the adult.

Orlando--- Is it possible to know anything with certainty, and to prove it?

Dumb question; the obvious answer is no. Even in science, using the research and development (R&D) model, necessary to achieve a maximal level of conclusion, the "scientific method" is frequently flawed with error leading to a false, at best questionable outcome.

Mom's Ghost--- As you became more socially savvy, new challenges presented for you to resolve.

My anxieties did not help. How I reacted to what happened to me made me feel joy (certainty)—when I correctly understood—or sadness (confusion)—when I didn't. External phenomena either set off a reasonable solution or added more stress to life, both consequences affecting my well-being.

But inside my brain, strong doubts launched superhero powers capable of strengths beyond Captain America in order to deal with joy and pain. Emanating from consequences of misreading others or misunderstanding my environment, I sensed the need to become savvier and more tolerant. My wisdom solidified with every new experience, as I moved closer to consecrate and balance Orlandito and Superboy to become Orlando.

Mom's Ghost--- You were growing up.

Orlando--- Fear drove the better part of my social interactions.

Mom's Ghost--- That happened as a consequence of you not understanding the implications and complexities of the events around you.

Orlando--- You think? Which was most significant? Picking up my Zundapp motorcycle at the dealer Christmas 1957, not certain of my ability to keep the "heavy bike" steady enough to move forward without falling sideways? Was that more exciting than meeting Capulí, the racehorse Dad bought me a year before for my tenth birthday, concerned with riding him? Or was it diving into the ocean from the jetty at Miramar Yacht Club (MYC), into bay water probably home to sharks? Or maybe walking up to my first crush, Teresita, at age ten to ask her to be my first girlfriend? Or hiding from you and Dad to smoke a

Kool cigarette? For certain, nothing compared to several failed attempted resuscitations of seventeen Dalmatian puppies Goya delivered in her first and only pregnancy. They all died from congenital malformations acquired from sibling sex. My breath stopped while each of theirs exhausted.

I know a lot of things appeared disgusting, like fish for dinner, my second-grade teacher's ugly toes showing through her sandals, cockroaches, rats, or toads running around, and Maco's assistant baseball coach spitting chewing tobacco. As I grew into a teenager, my culture was dauntingly transformed in parallel to changes in my environment. With each social interaction, I learned to distinguish things that were important to me from things that weren't.

I sensed the need to organize my thoughts to gain further understanding and awareness. I tried to imagine my future and plan for things to come. But I never imagined how big an impact my childhood would have years later as an adult.

My hormones were about to explode.

As I began writing this book, I sensed a need to explore "the reason behind the season," the psychology to explain why and how I became me. If you were authoring your story, wouldn't you want to know how and why you became you? I learned *transactional analysis* held the key.

Transactional analysis is a part of social psychology developed by the Canadian psychiatrist Eric Berne in 1958. It is based on the idea that people's early life experiences determine the decisions they will make later.

Orlando--- I played games that made me feel good and happy.

Mom's Ghost--- You loved playing the clown, and enjoyed watching friends and family laugh, feeling good about making them happy.

Orlando--- I still enjoy clowning around, chasing kids, especially my grandchildren, hiding, and suddenly appearing from a dark closet to shock them into laughter, like Jerry Lewis.

Berne described the game of "Stupid" as having the central concept of "I laugh with you at my own clumsiness and stupidity." He pointed out that *the player*---me, in this case--- has the advantage of lowering other people's expectations of our capacities, thus evading responsibility and work; but that he or she may still come through under pressure, like the proverbially stupid younger son. Said differently: make me accountable. It is a defense mechanism that buys time while we figure out our best shot at staying out of trouble---exposed to danger and punishment.

Orlando--- Was that me? It is amazing it took me fifty years to figure this one out.

God--- You bet.

Children grow up in a fantasy world, knowing extraordinarily little of what and who they want to be. Maybe who or what they do not want to be becomes clear sooner, as exposure to traumatic events begin to flood our senses at an incredibly early age.

Orlando--- According to Humberto, I was too sensitive to mom's directives, often throwing tantrums. "I don't think I should do it." "I don't want to do it." "You can't make me do it."

In order to survive, I had to figure out *"por dónde le entra el agua al coco?"* (How does water enter the coconut?)

Humberto's Ghost--- You did not realize it was all about safety and social accommodation to values and norms.

Orlando--- I did not wish to be a *boring* kid, too stupid, an idiot or moron, someone capable of causing damage to another person without experiencing personal gain (the definition of "stupid") or even worse causing damage to himself in the process.

I bought and read a lot of comic books. One of my favorites was Alfred E. Newman, a stereotyped image of stupidity.

Initially used in an editorial critical of abolishing the poll tax in the American South, the character depicted a young man who wants to vote but is too ignorant to understand what voting means. Thus, for me, appearing interesting and savvy was a major goal. I did not want to be like Newman.

Orlando--- Superboy, I created you, my superhero, so that I could find a way to be less stupid.

Superboy--- Your intent was to create me to prevent you from becoming our brother

Orlando--- Are you saying I saw Humberto as stupid?

Superboy--- You equated stupid with his inferiority complex, exhibited by his frequent attempts at being smarter, quicker, and more knowledgeable than others; to show off.

Orlando--- Exactly.

Superboy--- You felt it diminished him as a person you loved and respected, and in fact looked up to for his courage and abilities. Similar to what most children, other than the firstborn, experience when looking for a model or mentor to follow.

As I got older, my first dependency transfer, Mom to Humberto, evolved over a six-year period, from early middle childhood to puberty, materializing around the ages of seven through twelve, from primary education through middle school.

I found my second victim! It meant I chose to remain in a [stupid] victim role perfectly comfortable at the expense of another. He became the guide I would follow, I thought, for the rest of my life. Certain of my triumphant plan, I felt safe again; if I failed at becoming Superboy, I still had protection and support. I was dependent on my older brother to a degree understood by both of us, creating mutually desired codependency.

Orlando--- Humberto, do you agree?
Humberto's Ghost--- Gallego, I can't help you with that.

Unknowingly, during adolescence, the notion that while we think of ourselves as open-minded and objective, in fact our approach to ourselves is often filtered and even obscured by preexisting notions and ideas. I visualized, absorbed, and then embraced or rejected whatever influenced and guided my awareness.

Mom's Ghost--- What are the "blocked ideas" you are talking about? You did not have any "preexisting notions" or ideas. Which filters obscured your thinking?
Orlando--- Those I learned from you and Dad, and our circumstances.
Mom's Ghost--- Your upbringing? Our values? Our past experiences? Our behavior?
Orlando--- Yes! But mostly our circumstances.
Mom's Ghost--- What "circumstances?"

Memories theretofore hard to retrieve, so deeply subconscious they consolidated unnoticed along my life experience, became an all-pervasive influence that still today profoundly colors my adult relationships with people, and even myself. These ideas became part of my long-term memory---retrievable recall of [potentially] all my moments in time.

Dad's Ghost--- You said there were filters you used to block the pain of your reality. I know it was tough for all three of you at such an emotionally fragile age to face what happened to us in Cuba, Miami Beach, and Spain. You were exceptionally courageous.

Orlando--- Yeah, Dad, defense mechanisms I used to protect myself emotionally. I wasn't aware while it happened.

Mom's Ghost--- You finally grew up.

God--- All behavior---all ways of being and acting---are correlated to the context(s) from which we live our lives and observe both close relatives and strangers as they live theirs.

Dad's Ghost--- I can relate to that. We were immigrants, to whom contextual changes are a given.

Orlando--- That is exactly what I mean.

When these contexts became apparent and known, I began to see the unwitting process by which they were assembled, and the degree to which they governed my everyday life. I began to learn how to own my mistakes.

Dad's Ghost--- You were left, possibly for the first time, with a choice about who you were at that time, who you had been as a child and teen, and which adult would show up.

Everyone owns a "vicious circle," a human tendency to collapse what happened with the "story" we tell ourselves about what happened. This collapsing happens so fast it becomes hard to separate the two, and we think of them as one and the same. Almost immediately, and certainly over time, the story I told myself became "the way it was"---the reality I knew with certainty to be real. It limited what was "possible" in my life---everything, other than all things "I knew were true" --- robbing me of much joy and effectiveness.

My reality, perceived at any given time, became "my truth." It became "my story;" who I was willing to present myself to be; and who I would become. After all, decisions are based on personal conviction.

My favorite poem is the expression of all I believe and strived to achieve as I grew into an adult. The author is the most clear-minded leader I have read. It is my hope that I remain cognit enough to keep his wisdom central to both my convictions and actions:

> Your **beliefs** become your **thoughts,**
> Your thoughts become your **words,**
> Your words become your **actions,**
> Your actions become your **habits,**
> Your habits become your **values,** and
> Your values become your **destiny.**
> ---Mahatma Gandhi

When I separated what happened from my story or interpretation, I discovered that much of what I considered already determined, given and fixed, may in fact not be that way.

I found myself to be no longer limited by a finite set of options, and able to achieve what I wanted with new ease and enjoyment.

Situations that may have been challenging or difficult became fluid and open to change. I was able to join that group of people who are healthier in body and mind, simply feel better, and therefore be able to be happy and create happy lives.

Similar to most religious prayer, yoga offers these opportunities by organizing in worship groups that seek peace and enlightenment.

Dad's Ghost--- So interesting! Can you give me an example of these phenomenal insights?

Orlando--- I walked out on my family in the fall of 1996, the biggest mistake of many I ever made; my worst moment in time; the worst day in my life.

By April 1997 I was a mess.

Thankfully, things were about to get better. My best friend at the time, Humberto Dominguez, who practiced medicine at the same hospital where I worked as an anesthesiologist, called me on a Saturday morning to meet later that evening at a bar in Lake Mary, Florida for a drink.

After the third beer, as we vented worries and disappointments concerning our new "independent" lifestyle Humberto passed on the fourth---but I ordered mine. I sensed both Humberto and the bartender were perturbed. Witness to thousands of depressed drinkers sharing dreadful personal stories while imbibing excessive amounts of alcohol, and hoping to ease my pain, the bartender offered a lifeline.

The paper she handed me said "Landmark Education," followed by the phone number. Then, she said: "I think you should dial this number; they may help you." Next day, I registered with The Landmark Education Forum, which lasted three days.

On the third day, I learned to spot "the racket," an unproductive way of being or acting.

It explains *justifiable* complaints that something shouldn't be the way it is. Complaints may seem justified, even legitimate, but there is a certain payoff—real or imagined—some advantage or benefit received that reinforces the cycle of behavior.

At the same time, this way of being has steep costs, whether in our vitality, affinity, self-expression, or sense of fulfillment. We always lose something!

Once I recognized this pattern,---"my racket"---its costs, and how I kept the pattern in place, the choice to interrupt the cycle and discover new ways of interacting with others became clear. The racket helped me shift blame from me to others.

Happiness is talked about as almost a cute catchphrase, not a topic for serious scientific study. However, my state of satisfaction--my happiness---and optimism I desired, may not have been exclusively up to me, although it did reside within me. It was mostly a product of how I engaged in my world.

Orlando--- After the Forum, I finally achieved new levels of happiness, satisfaction, and fulfillment in areas that were important to me.

I learned that my brain---over 90%--- has the capacity to keep forever hidden in its depths inaccessible things we do not know that we don't know. Only the remaining 10% "workable knowledge"---memories we can retrieve---become accessible as things we know that we do not know (how to speak Chinese) and things we know that we know (how to speak English.)

These neurobiological connections, so common in all ages of humans, begin during childhood.

Orlando--- It took me another year---in preparation for a move to Syracuse, New York to train in a one-year anesthesiology fellowship program at SUNY---to fall back again into my depressed state, unable to see the light at the end of my dark tunnel.

Dad's Ghost--- I am sorry you had to go through something so painful.

Orlando--- Sometime in mid-August 1998, I was sitting in the SUNY at Syracuse Medical Center dining room across from a member of the neurosurgery associate staff. He noticed I could not eat my lunch, every swallow a challenge.

My Friend--- Why are you not eating? This is the third day I watch you fasting. What's wrong?

I began sharing my worries, my story, my racket, the vicious circle I felt unable to overcome.

Orlando--- My wife, Mary Carmen, was this---did that---made my life misery.

My friend--- What did you do?

Orlando--- Nothing!

My friend--- If you say so.

I was particularly likely to discount advice and proposed solutions to my problems and was apparently not looking to solve anything; I simply wanted *validation.* I walked back to my lonely apartment wondering the meaning of his words.

Within a week, I received a call from Orlando, Florida. Mary Carmen was on the phone, hysterical. One of our kids had overdosed and was now in the ER at a local hospital. After picking up my heart from the ground, praying to my Lord that he was still breathing, his brain still intact, my wife confirmed he was all right. I immediately requested a one-week leave to attend to this family emergency. My amazing department chairman conceded, and I was off to Orlando.

Thankfully, all was well, and remained mostly so through the following years. But now my cognition had shifted, recognizing, as a priority, mine, and my family's need to reunite. Still feeling our predicament was "all her fault," but overwhelmed by the reality of potential disaster, I called Mary Carmen to ask for forgiveness, something I have frequently, since then, done more than I am willing to admit and share.

Miraculously, with deep-felt fear, two months later, she came to Syracuse. She forgave me! We had a second honeymoon at Niagara Falls. I realized some of what happened may have been my doing; it was partially my fault!! My family was saved.

This behavior influenced my writing of this story, as I relate a child who had it too easy, was given a lot more than he deserved, and was pampered [luxury trap] with constant attention to his every need. Aware of this excess, both of my parents, especially Mother, would verbalize life lessons by giving advice on sinful (*avarice, selfishness, and pride*) behavior but remained intent on providing much more personal care than needed. Dad just gave me everything I asked for.

Tragically, some parents repeat this give-as-much-as-I-can conduct---rather than to reasonably provide all we can to those we love the most. Tough love is tough, so we bend to achieve secondary objectives with less than altruistic purposes---self-serving behavior that cements our racket. We feel better giving our kids all they want, even if we cannot afford it. They pick this up and learn the wrong lesson, that they can get anything they want, at any cost. Worse, that they can get anything they want...period.

One of my biggest challenges, in spite of all the toys I owned, was jealousy. I wanted everything everyone else owned. *Yo era un malcriado* (I was a spoiled brat.) My family and I set ourselves up for failure.

Chapter 12

Miramar

La Quinta Avenida (Fifth Avenue) was the principal boulevard in Miramar. I spent my middle childhood here, home to the famed Cubanacán Country Club.

Many of Havana's professionals and upper-middle-class residents owned property (no rentals) and lived there. Dozens of large mansions lined *5ta Avenida*, main thoroughfare in the *Marianao District*, sporting the most glamorous residential spaces in the Havana of the 1950s. Miramar Yacht Club was also there.

Pepe --- *Gallego, quieres ir a montar bicicleta? Escuché que Cuquita "la quincallera" tiene el último Superman que llegó ayer.* (Gallego, do you want to ride the bike? I heard Cuquita "the quincallera" has the latest Superman comic; it arrived yesterday.)
Orlando--- *Sí, vamos hasta la quincalla* (Yes, let's go to the quincalla.)

Cuquita owned the store. *La quincalla*, a convenience store, was our neighborhood's go-to place for all personal needs plus all trinket items. There, we bought gum and candy, toys, comic books, and school supplies. Cuquita also carried domestic articles, clothing, sewing materials and everyday necessities like soft drinks, paper towels, disposable plates and cups, plastic forks, spoons, and knives, and other items for use in parties and family outings.

Orlando--- We can play hide-and-seek.

Pepe--- That is great! But I want to go to baseball practice at the club. Maco Pérez is holding a clinic this weekend.

When we moved to Miramar and became members of the prestigious Miramar Yacht Club (MYC,) a new blessing appeared. The best baseball coach on the island, Maco Pérez, was the coach and general manager. Maco's real job was coaching the AAA national baseball team, the Cuban Sugar Kings.

MYC was a sports paradise by the ocean, featuring a fantastic marina and boathouse full of rowboats and canoes, kayaks, speedboats, and fishing yachts, sports fields (baseball, football, and soccer), a bowling alley, and squash and jai alai courts. Ping-Pong, billiards, and other table sports refined my motor skills. I was so good at these games that I fell victim to stereotyping and self-serving biases, believing that I was well above average on many a trait. I was way better. I was terrific, I was Superboy.

As a child athlete, I actively participated in an astounding variety of competitive sports: boxing (Culver Military Academy in Indiana), baseball (MYC), tennis (Graham Eckes School in Palm Beach, Florida), racquetball, track and field and football (Flamingo Park, South Beach, Florida), water skiing (pulled by Dad's "Zapato" speedboat), bowling, diving, sailing and rowing (MYC), spearfishing (SOBE), archery (Culver), motorcycle racing (Barlovento), horseback riding (Tarará, Cuba), and climbing tamarind (La Víbora) and Avocado trees (South Beach, Florida.)

As soon as I came home from school, I would run out of the house looking for my friends to play. Squash was at the top of my list. A racket-and-ball sport played by two or four players in a three-walled court, similar to racquetball and jai alai. Those who remember yesterday's Cuba and who were lucky enough to live a similar club atmosphere cannot forget the amazing life we enjoyed there. We usually drove up the circular driveway on our Zundapp motorcycles and went around it to check for friends.

Then, to the back parking area where we parked "the wheels." A walk to the club entrance brought the opportunity to say hi to the parking valet, *el parqueador*. According to one of our older club members, life at MYC was amazing for both, children, and adults.

Mother's Ghost--- Sometimes, there were people seated on the sofas and comfortable chairs in the lounge.

Orlando--- We could always stop to get a *Granadina---* a sweet and delicious soft drink prepared at the snack bar off the swimming pool.

Humberto's Ghost--- Or have a *"Miramar sandwich,"* ----a hearty ham and swiss , with a fried egg between two slices of white bread spread with mayo and mustard---everyone's favorite.

Miramar, as we called the club, had splendid athletes who were involved in several sports. Many of them were young men and women known on the island as fierce competitors, heroes to sports fans throughout the country. The club enthusiastically supported *los Caleteros* in all sports. MYC employed excellent coaches and directors as well. Swimming was supervised by a lifeguard, and swimmers were competitively trained under coach Carlos de Cubas, encouraging the swimmers to get in the water without fear.

Originally, when the Old Club was built in the twenties, the swimming pool was open to the ocean. *Lola la Puñales* -- a barracuda: her teeth were like knives---would share the pool with the swimmers, sometimes surfacing from under the raft. Her streamlined body looked elastic and powerful, shifting from flexible to stiff.

Orlando--- Yeah, she was dangerous. I did not like getting in the water when she was there.

Humberto's Ghost--- You never did. Besides, we were too young to compete at that level, so all we did was watch from the sand. Do not make up stories, Gallego.

Orlando--- I was really scared of this long, tubular fish with a very pointed snout filled with two rows of teeth, and small fins set back towards its crescent tail fin.

Humberto's Ghost--- She was shiny blue gray above, fading to silver and white below, with dark spots on her lower sides, and faint darker bars on the upper side.

Coach Cubas' Ghost--- A successful daytime ambush hunter that could swim in bursts of up to thirty-five miles per hour. Lola was no danger to humans on the raft.

Coach would often remind us Lola could mistakenly attack shiny objects or fish caught on spears. He would say, "if you see Lola showing her *puñales* (teeth) moving rapidly through the water, swishing her tail from side to side, get back on the raft." This tail action propels the fish much like sculling propels a boat.

During what we called the *Nortes* (our winter, carrying gusts of northeast winds), the coach would take the team to the swimming pool of another club, the Casino Español because high seas often invaded our open-ocean pool. As we approached the first swimming meets, *El Carnaval de Relevos* (the medley). I was certain we would win. Our excellent team included Luis Janes, Mayito Montalvo, Mauricio Astorga, Joaquín Fernández, Dicky Martín, Mayín Padrón, Ernestico Martín, Diego Roqué, and Manuel Fernández-Silva. I do not know if we often won because we were better trained or because we had more good swimmers.

My best friend at Miramar was Pepe Toraño. Another good friend was Jorge de Cardenas. He, and his brother, Mike, would borrow my Zundapp when I wasn't looking. It made me mad for a few minutes but then I was fine after a good laugh.

In the evening, our parents and friends would meet in the lounge, or the dining room, or the terrace, or the bar. Many opportunities existed at the club for members of all ages to have lots of fun.

Those parties! My parents enjoyed the *Debutantes Ball*, held in celebration of fifteen-year-old (*quinceañeras*) girls coming out into "social adulthood," the *Fiestas Guajiras* (country-style parties), the parties given by the *"yachtistas"* (yacht people), the *Masquerade Ball*, and those celebrating the coming of the New Year. Oh, and the parties in the skating rink, and, finally, the most endearing, *las fiestas de los niños* (the children's parties) *con piñatas*: competition pitted every kid, with eyes blindfolded, taking turns at banging the large, candy-filled pâpier-maché box with a stick so all its yummy contents could fall on the ground to see who would collect more treats.

So much to remember!

Mom's Ghost--- *El club era el sitio más seguro para que ustedes jugaran.* (The club was the safest place for you to play).

Baseball was king. *"La pelota es un deporte de equipo donde nueve jugadores con un guante en la mano impiden que el equipo al bate anote carreras,"* ("Baseball is a team sport where nine players with a glove in their hand prevent the batting team from scoring runs"), Maco Pérez would exclaim. Maco taught "the four corners" drill.

Maco--- Catching and throwing a baseball, down to the ground or up as a flyball, *center-back, center-forward, right-back, and right-forward* develops eye-hand coordination and muscle memory.

Dad and Mom often attended practice, an opportunity to show off our skill during a play colored by an extra step to make it appear *lijosa* (dramatic)---more difficult to achieve greater impact. Typically, Maco and Humberto verbalized most of what I heard.

Maco--- The most important person on a team is called the pitcher, who throws a ball to the second most important person on the team, the catcher. Everyone needs to be watching the pitcher and the catcher, to see where the pitch goes, what the batter does, and be ready--- know beforehand what you will do next.

Humberto--- Pay attention, Gallego. Stop looking at the girl on the sidelines!

Team Verde de pelota 1957, winner of the Club Championship.
Kneeling: A. López, Orlando García, Arístides Fernández Abril,
Pepe Toraño and J.M. Espinosa

Chapter 13
Ana María Is Born

During our last year at Miramar, one of the best things that ever happened to me occurred on August 25, 1956, the most surprising day in my life, my little sister's birth, ten years and one day following mine. We named her Ana María. As I recall, I was having the time of my life at my tenth birthday party when my term-pregnant mother "disappeared." *Se la tragó la tierra* (the earth swallowed her.) No one would explain to me why she was gone, except for Aunt Chely (Tía Tá), always watching out for my mood and safety, making sure I understood the world around me.

Orlando--- Tía Tá, dónde está Mamá? (Tía Tá, where is Mom?)

Chely--- *Fué al hospital a traerte un bebé.* (She went to the hospital to bring you a baby.) *Es hembra!* (It's a girl!)

She really did not know for certain. In 1956 there was no ultrasound; the newborn's sex was a surprise to all.

We went to bed for a few hours, and then it happened. Early morning August 25, 1956, Tía Tá brought Humberto and me to the hospital to meet her. I stood there in amazement. A tingle surged throughout my whole body. A rush of excitement I had never felt before in my life.

This tiny little thing was suddenly mine; I claimed possession immediately. When my eyes hit her angelic little body, they froze up, and I couldn't think or acknowledge anything else around me. I began basking in a pleasurable experience I wished never to end; being totally satisfied with "my present" and enjoying the present.

The world seemed to stop, hold its place in time, just for that perfect moment. She is kind of weird, I thought, so small and wrinkled. While she slept, I stared at this precious little angel. My hands quivered as I slowly reached down to touch her little fingers and feel the softness of her skin. I ran the tips of my fingers very gently across her smooth face, and right away, I fell in love.

Then, my brother said: "You can wake her up and hold her." I was ecstatic. I was finally going to meet her! As I held her, I stared into her gorgeous brown eyes and knew instantly that I would love and cherish her forever with all my heart. Anita was *edible,* her baby fat rounded her arms like a sausage. Her legs, likewise, appeared from under the dress screaming "bite me." I loved to pinch her butt and cheeks and play all day long. I couldn't stop kissing her, holding her, making funny faces to draw her attention hoping for a response, an imitation. She filled everyone's heart with joy, especially mine.

Ana Maria lived in Cuba from birth to New Year's Day 1959. She left her country for good at two years and four months of age. As I was ten years her elder, we sadly did not spend that much time together, but she always ran to me for a hug whenever she saw me coming.

Anita, as I later called her, was always playfully seeking attention. When she did not, we would all feel worried, approaching her from behind to call "peek-a-boo." She would jump back and laugh, just like when she was tickled. Always kept clean and perfumed, bathed with French shampoo followed by liberally splashed cologne, dressed like a doll, and pampered by all. Rare was the time someone was not holding her. All this attention made her feel special, thus inducing habits she learned and expected, the beginning of her own luxury trap.

Years later, in Madrid, Spain, Anita had her First Communion. Dressed in a white sparkle organza fabric, her garment ended just above the knees. She was twelve years old. Ana Maria attended catholic school in Madrid. Later, she married René, one of my childhood's best friends. Within a couple of years, she filed for divorce. He became Lex Luthor.

Chapter 14
Culver Military Academy

Woodcraft Division 2

From 1950 to 1956 we listened to, breathed, tasted, and smelled every game the Yankees played. We memorized their roster, role-played their positions, talked up their assets, emulated their feats, and became them. So, when June 1957 arrived and it was time to travel to NYC, a first stop before summer camp near Chicago we were only thinking about Yankee Stadium. I was eleven years old.

As we prepared for the trip, Humberto and I were shown pictures of a military school in northern Indiana called Culver

Military Academy (George Steinbrenner's alma mater,) which appeared to offer all kinds of fun activities and sports. Dad did not tell us why we were going to spend time abroad, but later I learned the reason. Havana was no longer safe because Fidel Castro's urban guerrilla was snatching rich kids and those from families that held close relationships with government, to hold them for ransom.

Not all ended well. So, my parents were anxious to send us to study in the US. Shortly after arriving at La Guardia Airport, we took a taxi and checked into the Waldorf Astoria.

The Waldorf was world renowned as the most luxurious hotel in New York City. It was hard to keep up with us, so Mom stopped running after our tails and started praying for our return to her once we had concluded our playful disappearances inside the hotel. We visited all the typical tourist classics one by one: the Empire State Building, the Statue of Liberty, a boat ride on the Hudson, Saint Patrick's Cathedral on Fifth Avenue, the stores on Forty-second Street and Fifth Avenue, the Broadway theaters, and a horse-drawn carriage ride in Central Park. Mother was pressing to leave for the hotel to pick up the luggage and head for Penn Station to board the train to Chicago, then on to South Bend, and finally, Culver.

Dad--- Time to go.
Superboy--- Where?
Mom--- Chicago.
Humberto--- Wait a minute, aren't we going to Yankee Stadium?

We pulled on Dad's coat and grinded our teeth and grunted: "Yankee Stadium, Papá!" We threw a tantrum---*perreta*. I always knew he would not let us down; never did. Soon thereafter, we boarded the No. 4 train bound for Woodlawn to the Bronx. As we exited at the 161st Street/Yankee Stadium Station, our hearts were pounding. We ran down the subway stairs to the street level, Dad trying to keep up with us. We crossed the street without looking as we ran from the train. We had the stadium in front of us, then the open gates. Pleas and demands coming at machine-gun speed from both of us was too much to bear. "C'mon, Dad!" Now we were yell-pleading, as we ran into the stadium.

The ramps up to the first level, a race against the clock, reaching back in time, running to younger years, seeking voices and sounds of yesterdays.

Then, we ran to our left, our pounding hearts rushing blood to and from the brain and both legs, leaving the gut bloodless. There it was! A light of sunshine through the round wall on the right.

If I had a hundred pages to write, I would describe all the details, the blades of grass... but let this suffice: we knew it was seconds to Heaven.

The sun exploded its light through the open gates leading into the rows of chairs and isles--- it came out like a burst of fire, blown out of the sky into our baseball park. Then, the greenest grass I had ever seen. Our hearts racing at extremely high speed suddenly stopped. For a few seconds, there was no blood flow.

In anticipation of this miracle, our bodies entered the bleachers, our souls the grass; and there they were, all their ghosts dressed in white with blue pinstriped uniforms, our Yankees in position: Catcher Yogi Berra behind home plate, with a great big smile. Bill Skowron on first base; Billy Martin on second base; Andy Carey on third base; Gill McDougald at shortstop, a position previously played by one of my favorites, Phil Rizzuto, retiring to become a radio and TV broadcaster. Elston Howard was in left field; Mickey Mantle centerfield (my favorite player of all time)---Joe DiMaggio had retired in 1951; Hank Bower was in right field, and Whitey Ford was on the pitcher's mound, the lefty getting ready to deliver a killer curveball.

Our hearts filled with gratitude and a satisfied soul, so alive and thankful to the best father in the world, we took the subway back to Penn Station. That afternoon, we left for Chicago.

We had reservations at The Palmer House, a given, the best hotel in town. At dinner that night our table was served by two waiters, one standing by the table the whole meal to refill cold water to our glasses by just looking his way. Dressed in Redcoat, a scarlet tunic---military garments used widely by most regiments of the British Army, Royal Marines, and some colonial units within the British Empire, from the seventeen to the twentieth centuries: they marched to and fro bringing our five-course meal. The dinner plate in the middle, dinner fork and salad fork to the left of the plate, butter knife with the blade facing the dinner plate and the spoon on the outside to the right of the plate. The next day, the train to Culver.

Culver Woodcraft Camp offered a six-week, activity-based summer camp designed for youth ages nine to fourteen. Many challenging sports activities, including some neither one of us had any previous exposure to—river-rafting, fencing, archery, swimming in the freezing lake water, and boxing, to name a few—promised a magnificent opportunity to enjoy a great summer experience.

We arrived by train from Chicago in the second week of June 1957. A late afternoon 'T' stopped at Culver Station and moved directly to The Culver Inn on Lake Maxinkuckee, an old red brick and stone building that served as a hotel and restaurant for parents and visitors. I recall the brochure we picked up in the Admissions Office. "Culver Military Academy in northern Indiana, founded in 1902, and Culver Summer Schools and Camps added later to a fun-filled, naturally beautiful 1,700-acre setting where young people develop positive self-esteem through personal accomplishment and self-discipline, are our goal."

The brochure added: "Our mission is to educate the students for leadership and responsible citizenship in society by developing and nurturing the whole individual—mind, spirit, and body—through integrated programs that emphasize the cultivation of character, delivered in a high challenge, high support environment for learning leadership skills that improve personal confidence."

Humberto was twelve and I was eleven. Woodcraft Camp offered more than eighty elective courses and activities. We couldn't wait to jump into the new adventures before us.

Then, tragedy struck. Shortly after we arrived at camp, following sign-in, we moved out of the administration building to a large area of grass and camper tents. The academy guidance counselor assigned to us for orientation, Colonel Parks, gave us the scoop on the sleeping quarters.

Colonel Parks--- The A-frame cabins are equipped with ceiling fans and screened windows all around. Woodcrafters sleep practically in the open air. Each camper has a center bin, wardrobe, and athletic bin assigned to them for personal items.

He was tall and quite imposing, wearing multiple ribbons and medals attached to his shirt pockets, pins screwed into his navy-blue uniform, mostly on the cap and lapel, sporting awareness of his military category and a big contagious smile. All our personal items had been neatly folded and arranged by Mom before departing Havana, and placed in two large wood trunks, one for each of us.

Colonel Parks--- Cabins house up to twelve campers, Woodcrafters and a counselor. Each group of four or five cabins comprises a unit, which also includes a head counselor and two to three assistant counselors. The head counselor is your main point of contact throughout the summer. You must always keep a positive attitude, especially while sharing personal experience with other campers.

As he spoke, I felt a knot in my stomach, sensing the dreaded moment of separation from Mother was nearing. I held on tight to her dress, as the Colonel pointed to a group of student campers chatting nearby.

"Dan clung to her in speechless gratitude, feeling the blessedness of mother love, — that divine gift which comforts, purifies, and strengthens all who seek it."
—Louisa May Alcott, *Jo's Boys*

Panic attacks involve sudden feelings of terror that strike without warning. People experiencing a panic attack may think they are having a heart attack, are dying, or are going crazy. My discomfort was more separation anxiety than anything else. I dared not speak a word while Humberto kept tugging at me the way Mom would if she needed my attention. Suddenly, Humberto looked at Colonel Parks and spoke out of turn.

Humberto--- Attitudes are basic expressions of approval or disapproval---when we are in favor of or against something we like or dislike. I hope we like those campers you are referring to.

I could sense something bad was about to happen. It scared me; everyone else appeared to be okay with it. I kept holding on to Mom's dress, nervously moving closer to her. Finally, Humberto tightened his grip on my hand, separating me from Mom, and began dragging me toward the boys in uniform.

Humberto--- *Vamos, Gallego! Corre, vamos, vamos!* (Come on, Gallego! Run, let's go!)

As we left Mom behind, I turned to look and wave, but she was gone. That's when it happened. We approached the campers who appeared to be chatting, joking around, laughing out loud, and just having a good time. In a New York minute, their attitude turned. I noticed it, and I know Humberto did as well. I briefly remembered Miss Ledo's words: "Your interests must be triggered by the wish to communicate with American kids. Both of you will approach several children who will want to play with you; be vigilant of their intent."

Both they and we immediately faced a new challenge. To adapt, perceive, comprehend, and quickly interpret the changing world around us, particularly each other's potential action toward one another was now a priority. As we construed a sudden change in intent, subjecting reality and its effect on personal safety and significance, there was no time to find reason or explain what, how, or why this was happening. We needed clarity on the next step.

Mom and Dad and the Colonel had spent days talking up the friendships and camaraderie to embrace from other children at camp. But the kids we approached, standing on a grassy knoll, suddenly realized we did not look like them; we were shorter, darker, walking weird--- obviously not the usual sight to see two boys approaching holding hands!

As proud as he was, trying always to put out his big brother's chest in the presence of imminent ridicule, Humberto sensed this was not the moment to show strength. It was neither a time to go forward, insecure about our poor English-language skills, nor slowly retreat heads down in shame. I was not about to bend and relinquish my superpower character afforded by the certainty of my role as Superboy. I thought: "I must not allow us to get too close, risking appearing a merry mockery of all I held dear as my strength represented those I wished to become."

Limited by our bounded rationality, Humberto acted quickly, adapting to what appeared to be a situation out of control: my brother took off in a new direction. Toward the cabins he ran, still with my hand in his. I ran with him, save my arm from being torn off, to the back of the woods near a wood-and-canvas tent that housed campers, still empty awaiting the first residents. We sat on the ground next to a cabin. I felt the soil soften and my pants wet in warm liquid, urine running through my underwear onto my thigh. It was not the first time for me. I suffered nocturnal enuresis in Cuba for years. It would persist a bit longer.

For the next two weeks, peeing in bed required an early rise to wash and dry the bedsheets before the morning first call, bugle trumpet sounding a warning that campers must prepare to assemble for formation, a task only Superboy could accomplish. A march to Chow Hall for a wholesome and nutritious breakfast would follow. I always looked forward to a super-hot serving of steel-cut oatmeal with raisins, cinnamon, and honey.

Nevertheless, as we marched, a painful emotion caused by the belief that I could be perceived as inferior or unworthy of affection or respect engulfed my thinking. I was overwhelmed by it and felt so poorly about myself, embarrassed and humiliated, that my self-respect weakened. I was weighed down by a consciousness of guilt and impropriety. It was also cold as hell! Those Indiana summer nights brought temperatures thirty and forty degrees Fahrenheit lower than those we previously experienced in Cuba. The wind blowing from the lake did not help.

Dad's Ghost--- I'm sure it was tough, but you did what was right. I am proud of you.
Orlando--- I struggled.
Superboy--- I tried to help you.

I was sharing my cabin with another boy who slept on a nearby bunk. I couldn't allow him to know I had wet the bed, ashamed to share the smell of urine; I would have done anything to prevent it. There was no other solution but to take the wet sheets out of the cabin at 4 a.m. to wash them in a huge tent housing the troopers' common sinks and showers. Then, pick them up and strain each---just the area wet with urine---and hang them to dry on nearby bushes. Then go back to the tent, lay down on the mattress for about an hour and remake the bed at 6:30 am---with cold, wet sheets before anyone else woke up.

This went on for about two weeks, when Superboy suddenly realized it was no longer happening. The tide had turned. I was now one of them, but my pride had been injured.

Behavior is impacted by certain traits that vary from person to person and can frequently influence or be triggered by new actions and new behaviors. We must resolve these triggers in order to act "normal" according to local norms and behavioral patterns. I believe that event in Culver, on the first contact with those who appeared as friends but quickly became foes, turned the tide that we surfed, pedaled, and paddled for the rest of a good part of our lives.

Humberto's Ghost--- Okay, let us say you're right. But you know why we ran, right?

Orlando--- Sure, I know.

Humberto's Ghost--- So, it wasn't just because I was afraid for your safety only; as a matter of fact, I was also scared shitless. I didn't know what to expect! It was better to play it safe.

Orlando--- I know. I'm not blaming you.

Humberto's Ghost--- I'm just saying! Confrontation was a risk we could not afford to take.

Many issues regarding shameful behavior were hidden from the other campers, both inside and outside the cabin. Each cabin slept four, two campers on one side of a dividing wood wall cutting the tent in two halves without reaching the ceiling, and two on the other side. One of the two boys sleeping on the opposite side sometimes stood on the footboard of his bed to look over the wall to call us. It was either for conversation and bragging about some competitive sports achievement or to show us his penis, significantly larger than the other three. I confess to have looked at it with amazement and often with lust directed at packing one myself, i.e., owning one.

This experience was quite confusing, as I pondered sex preference. It presented a dichotomous debilitating feeling of divergent fondness or appetite for either gender, a greater liking for one alternative over another. I was twelve years old and liked girls, but this experience was weird and made me uncomfortable.

As we moved up from Culver Military Academy Summer Camp through Graham-Eckes School in Palm Beach, on to Miami Beach Senior High School and eventually into medical school in Madrid, Spain, I saw in Humberto the fear of failure shown that first day on Culver ground. The decision he made to run away from imminent danger, risking any one of those boys putting his manhood into question, seemed the right thing to do at that time. However, he knew that I knew he chickened out. I never called him on that one.

Humberto's Ghost--- I refused to change who I was. You, on the other hand, became a chameleon. I watched you adapt to different environments at the expense of your ego.

Orlando--- As a teenager, you only dated Latin girls, refused to be "Americanized," never spoke English without a Spanish accent, and put forth a grandiose personality. Your immense ego ruled your behavior. I, on the other hand, decided to be just like those boys---adapt.

I identified with my new environment. I adapted. My spoken English would be so perfect that no one would ever notice I was a foreigner. My mannerisms, favored sports, music preferences, and game style would be as American as apple pie. I wanted to change from the "rich kid" persona I was in Cuba, to those Midwestern unpretentious middle schoolers who just wanted to have fun. That is the way I *chose* to view the impact diversity presented us with that day.

Although my new world did not really change me significantly, it felt like giving up who I was to that moment---changing into a new persona. I realized that I could save myself the grief and pain of those who are paralyzed by adaptation. We both had our own ego to protect, and each found a distinctly personal road to balance who we were against the demands imposed by our circumstances. As Orlando began to role-play a new self, Superboy, serenity replaced my anxiety.

The impact this new country would have was unpredictable. Our parents chose to protect us from physical danger at home, so they shipped us abroad. Attending a Midwestern military school within the United States, sensitized us to the new environment to a much greater degree than either our parents or we expected.

Whatever took place in that unexpected process of approach-perception-arrival and the subsequent "fight or flight" moment of departure from clear and present danger, left those boys and us wondering what happened. I asked myself: "Why didn't Mother foresee this terrible moment?"

Chapter 15:

El Biltmore

My last Cuban *barrio* was also located near the ocean. We only lived there eighteen months, losing our home to the Castro Revolution.

After moving to El Biltmore, we were blessed with the means to pay for two sleep-in maids and our nanny (Cachita), a *chauffeur* (Luis), and a chef (Modesto). It was not like that in La Víbora or Miramar, our previous neighborhoods. Those beautiful brown and black persons---*los criados* ("The Help") working at our home---had families of their own. They were good, honest people, committed to their family and the health of their children; it was their duty. But, not having experienced them in their private world, I wondered if they practiced Santería.

El Biltmore Home

My childhood was impacted by a multiplicity of significant disasters: political crime, the Second World War, the nuclear bomb, racism, questionable morals, deceitful close relationships, and distorted religion and faith. Nevertheless, my parents made sure I saw only the good, effecting a positive philosophical view of myself and my surroundings. Mother's advice, "Look upon your life with positivity rather than counting the ways God hasn't blessed you," stuck with me throughout the years, helping me to stay focused on my blessings.

My Family / Goya & Rebert

Maybe it was "instant gratification" that drove my frequent desires and demands, or the excess of toys and frequent "surprises" we received from family and friends, especially during Christmas, Los Reyes Magos, and birthdays. *Yo era un "malcriado"* (I was naughty.) On my tenth birthday, I asked Dad for a motorcycle, which Mother immediately turned down, so he asked me if there was anything else, and I said: "A horse." He brought me to a huge stable just outside Havana. The track was operational during the winter months, and many of America's top stables brought their best horses to Oriental Park Racetrack to compete. It opened in 1915, operated by a friend, the owner of the Havana-American Jockey Club of Cuba.

The owner offered Dad the best he had in the stable. I overheard the man say to Dad, "This horse was sired by a famous thoroughbred, Nashua, winner of the Kentucky Derby in 1955." At the end of his 1956 season, after thirty career races with a record of 22–4–1, Nashua was retired to stand at stud, the second horse to earn more than $1 million. As we walked the stables, this amazing animal looked at us and, I swear, smiled. I named him Capulí. He won every race he entered, but after we took him home, he never raced again.

I got my motorcycle the following Christmas 1957. My Zundapp was specifically adapted to my height and weight. The front frame curved down from under the handlebars to the pedals, to allow my short legs to jump onto and reach a flat surface after a short run to move the bike forward. Once off the ground, as I stood and hurled myself on to the seat, I gained the necessary balance for forward motion as I opened the throttle.

Mom--- Humberto, my husband, I cannot believe you want your kids dead! You bought these two "motos" last year without consulting me first. You know I would never agree.

Unfortunately, this magnanimously profligate behavior did not parent a child accountable for financial responsibilities and committed to engage in obligations typified by thrift and constraint. To the contrary, it transferred a sense of unlimited resources, a big-spender mentality that forever affected Humberto and me.

It also triggered a *compulsive* shopper behavior, adding impulsivity and carelessness to every purchase, every dream, in order to sustain our "luxury trap." Years later, practicing medicine in Orlando, Florida, I walked into a Acura dealership and purchased four of the five automobiles in the showroom.

The fifth was an NSX worth $100,000. Even today, it is difficult to turn my back on the compulsion to purchase things. It still controls my life, like a gambling addiction.

Superboy led a motorcycle boys gang of sorts, gathered around motorbikes, close friends with compatible tastes and mutual interests who frivolously enjoyed the "safe" neighborhood. A nearby new development, Barlovento---later Marina Hemingway—was my private Daytona Speedway. With paved streets and sidewalks, underground electrical and plumbing, light posts, and street signs already up in the new development, the ocean breeze from Cuba's Atlantic coast blew in new dry sand needed to provide a shallow street cover, perfect for a sliding, exhilarating motorcycle race experience.

Not quite faster than the speed of light, nor with a strength to lift it off the ground, I and my Zundapp German motorcycle took off on Barlovento's empty streets (not a single house yet built) as lightning propelled from the starting signal's lowering of the flag. I sped over sandy roads and moved laterally to rock side to side as fast as I could, passing my friends' bikes as I opened the throttle leaving each turn and entering the straightaway.

Focused on the checkered flag and the winner's circle, other competitors lost the race--- to them an all-or-nothing event; there was nothing else but winning in their mind. For Superboy, the thrill came from every second-to-second breath filled with ocean salt and water, the gentle sounds of soft waves breaking into the marina, and the roar of the engines cogwheeling RPMs.

The thrill of the road I experienced firsthand transferred to professional car racing as well. When I was eleven years old, I watched Formula One racing in Havana's Grand Prix (El Gran Premio de La Habana, 1957), becoming a lifelong fan of Argentine great Juan Manuel Fangio. He dominated the first decade of Formula One racing, winning the World Drivers' Championship five times.

The Batista government had established the non-Formula One Cuban Grand Prix in 1957. Fangio won the 1957 event: his picture driving the race-winning 250F Maserati around a turn at the Malecón portion of the bay on the circuit hangs today on the wall above my master bed's headboard. He had set the fastest times during practice for the 1958 race. His stardom would lead to a desperate situation.

On February 23, 1958, two unmasked gunmen of Fidel Castro's 26th of July Movement entered the Hotel Lincoln in Havana and kidnapped Fangio at gunpoint. The motive was pure: By capturing the biggest name in motorsport, the rebels were showing up the government and attracting worldwide publicity to their cause. But despite the shocking news spreading across the globe, *el Presidente Batista* would not be outdone and ordered the race to continue as usual while a crack team of police hunted down the kidnappers. Uncle Orlando ordered roadblocks at intersections and assigned guards to private and commercial airports and all competing drivers. The rebels released Fangio after twenty-nine hours.

I felt pride each time I listened to the story as Mom told it to her friends and Dad. She did not like for Humberto and me to repeat things we heard at home, but we spread, among our friends, the police action as a story of Uncle Orlando achieving superhero power and using it to save the life of the greatest racecar driver ever. It fit right in with the drama filling the dreams I embraced of being, myself, a superhero.

Chapter 16

Graham-Eckes School

Dear God,
Grant me the serenity
to accept the things I cannot change,
the strength to change the things I can,
and the wisdom to know the difference.
--- *The Serenity Prayer*

Graham-Eckes School was founded in 1926 in Daytona Beach by half-sisters Inez Graham and Evelyn Eckes. It was what is now called a college prep school, and it taught students from kindergarten through high school. In 1941, it moved to a three-and-a-half-acre ocean-to-inland waterway "Mar-a-Lago" known as Oheka.

The school building itself had been a mansion designed by Maurice Fatio. The dormitories and tennis courts were added later. It remains one of Florida's oldest private schools. Graham-Eckes, the town's only high school, was "Palm Beach" down to the silverware. Its three hundred or so students wore immaculate summer and winter uniforms, broke for afternoon tea, had formal dinners every day and cotillions every week, and learned strict codes of social graces and honor. Many went on to Ivy League schools.

The day we arrived, in the fall of 1958, Humberto and I sat down with the guidance counselor. As she reviewed our academic history and performance at La Salle, she saw evidence I had completed sixth grade (to catch up to Humberto) by taking private classes with Mr. Mederos in Havana over the summer. We were positioned to enter seventh grade, but when we offered the subject transcripts, there was a pause by the student admissions counselor as she considered whether to accept or reject this entry level.

Here was the problem: Cuba's school system, *Bachillerato* (Bachelor), and the US systems of middle and high school do not have a clear equivalency. Both high school and *Bachillerato* end with grade 12. The difference lies in that the former requires four years following middle school (seventh and eighth grades) while the latter structures five years following seventh grade.

At that point, Humberto and I had six years left to graduate from either school system. In a numerical format, the current grade we were both scheduled to enter was seventh. My academics may have said one thing, but my body and my emotions exposed another. I had just turned a "small" eleven, too immature to start seventh grade. I had already studied, urgently completed, and passed a contracted sixth grade in the summer, so I really thought I needed to enter sixth grade to strengthen the subjects while my English vocabulary grew.

Amazingly, the adults in the room (Mother and the counselor) became confused. Mother insisted that Cuba's education surpassed the one in the US, and this pressured the school administrators to go even further. Rather than signing me up for the sixth grade, where I felt I belonged emotionally, the counselor placed both of us in the seventh grade.

Now, in seventh grade, we were two years away from the ninth grade, high school freshmen. Mother's dream to see us walk up to the podium together in cap and gown was moving in the right direction. However, we were too short to fit in---not only Cuban (shorter stature than American) but also one year (Humberto) or two (me) younger than the rest of the class. Even the girls towered over both of us. They looked at us as geniuses, and we at them as giants.

Humberto's Ghost--- *Te acuerdas, Gallego?* "*Caballo grande, ande o no ande!*" Do you remember, Gallego? "get a big horse, whether it walks or not!")

This popular saying can have a variety of meanings. Bigger is always better, they say. Used as a criticism of those who acquire or seek large things guided only by the desire for ostentation, without looking at its usefulness, beauty, elegance... for most Cuban males it meant you can show off a tall woman and her corporal attributes better than a short one.

Orlando--- On Sundays, we attended lessons on how to serve tea.

Mother's Ghost--- This experience will be useful if some day you travel to England. When you come home, I look forward to being served tea by my sons.

Humberto's Ghost--- I hated it. I'll never know why the school did not have a baseball team, focusing instead on sophisticated elegance and manners.

Professional chefs prepared meals, and students were told to watch the butler because he epitomized the perfect gentleman. Maids stayed busy cleaning rooms. The school had a sailing club, fencing club, and every language club imaginable. It had its nurse, its bookstore, its unmistakable *cachet*. The dress code, particular fashion depending on the era, put girls in shirtwaist dresses, or in blazers and skirts and guys in slacks and ties. It was strict, strict, strict.

The local Catholic church, St Edward's on 144 North County Road, has been called "the most beautiful church" in Palm Beach, and remembered for its "splendid architecture, a storied congregation, and simply magnificent interior." It was (and is) located across the street from the legendary Green's Drug Store, a pharmacy luncheonette established in 1938, where customers enjoy good food and thick milk shakes while they wait for the prescriptions.

A couple of my buddies, Humberto, and I would sneak out of the church during mass, cross the street and go to the coffee shop next to Green's owned by Joe DiMaggio's uncle, obviously a die-hard Yankees fan. Dozens of black-and-white pictures of Yankees players in pinstripes filled the café's walls, primary stimulus for us, rabid Yankees fans. My favorite breakfast was simply American coffee and English muffins smeared with butter and strawberry jelly.

I also cannot forget the jokes we played on the Spanish teacher. One of many examples: After a couple of months of Sunday treks to church, Carlos Pires, one of the Cuban students, came up with a prank. Being one of the older in the group, he convinced the rest of us to swear to the teacher that we had converted to Islam, thus we could no longer attend mass on Sunday.

Humberto and I struggled to fit in at Graham-Eckes, where we were in the minority but not alone. A small group of six or seven, we and our Cuban friends relied on each other for safety and community and felt relieved to be able to speak Spanish together. Unlike when interacting with the elitist American students, who showed racism and prejudice toward us despite our social status in Cuba, within our tiny Cuban circle, culture was not a barrier. At first, all of the Cuban students were our close friends but that would change upon our return.

Part 4

Escape From Havana

Chapter 17

Facing a New Beginning

I do not remember my brother's state of mind at the time we left Palm Beach and flew back home to enjoy Christmas with our family. My feelings were different than when leaving summer camp at Culver the previous summer. I knew how much I suffered at Graham-Eckes, victim of prejudice and racism. More than a few lessons from many disappointments, and dreams shattered---built around belonging to a "superior" society. I knew better now. I knew that I was not accepted by the American elite, nor would I ever be. Coming home was a huge relief, the happiest day of my life, December 20, 1959.

----A lot more pain was still to come.

Christmas came and went; an incredible family reunion filled with love and stories about school and the American lifestyle. I tried to hide my pain, even from myself, giving florid accounts of positive experiences, challenging sports, and amazing social events among socialites. Palm Beach was, after all, a world-renowned home to the richest on the globe. The family was delighted by our stories and felt proud that they had the means and courage to send us there.

However, they were kept from many unsavory experiences that we suffered during our first three months at the school. Humberto and I were bullied by several American students who also impinged pain on other smaller children. One of them was named MacDonald. He was scary. I saw him punch a kid in the mouth knowing that he had braces. Profuse bleeding presented a horrible scene that I re-lived in nightmares during numerous nights while at Palm Beach, praying he would not choose me as his next victim. Things would get a lot worse upon our return in January.

New Year's Eve 1958 arrived. The day began so uneventfully that I have no recollection of it. I know that all preparations were toward getting ready for the New Year's Eve party at Abuela Rita's house; we were all together, almost. Soon thereafter, it would become brutally clear why the men were missing from the family reunion. It would also become the most important day of my life.

That night, I itched with sadness and uncertain emotion knowing the trip back to school was imminent. Palm Beach was waiting. We were scheduled to fly back to school on January 6. This upset me terribly because this is Three Kings Day, when Melchor, Gaspar, and Balthasar bring gifts to baby Jesus in Bethlehem. Not that my Catholic school's religious teachings had enough impact on me to cement my faith in God; no, this was not the reason for my "misfortune," but rather the thought of not getting my gifts from *"Los Reyes Magos"* (The Magic Kings). Cuba being a predominantly Christian populace, Catholic theology ruled over laic institutionalized dogma, which Santa Clause epitomized on Christmas Eve by bringing gifts to children throughout the Western world. Thus, we received more gifts on January 6 than on Christmas Day.

Our parents had sent us to study abroad to shield us from the violence in Havana spun by Castro's revolutionary forces, the urban guerrillas. With effort to win the war against the "evil" forces of a "dictator," i.e., Fulgencio Batista, Castro's city fighters planted explosives in movie theaters, schools, and sidewalks, provoking panic, and death among innocent people.

They also, as part of their terror tactics, snatched children of the ruling class and wealthy families from playgrounds, schools, and neighborhoods to then demand ransom in exchange for their lives. My family, my uncles in particular, was part of that government elite. We were the "privileged few." My parents were willing to take every precaution to prevent this from happening to my brother and me.

As a twelve-year-old, nothing in my wildest dreams could have provided a clue to an event that would twist destiny in a knot to tighten and choke all of Cuba's hopes for a better future, one that would consume every drop of life from its people, one that no one but a few of us saw coming: the triumph of the Revolution. This event would bring unimaginable pain and catastrophe to Cuba. Although most of the Cuban population was against Batista, whom they saw as a ruthless assassin who perpetrated terror upon his people, there was much they did not know. Corruption and tyranny were often cited in parallel with his regime, and those who felt that way were right.

Nevertheless, communism was threatening the country. Fidel Castro, a proven assasin when he was a law student, had become, with his brother, Raul, a member of the Communist Party in the late 1940s. There was a global struggle that pitted fascism against communism. An ally of the United States, Batista, and his followers, chose the anticommunist side of the political spectrum. Although his choice brought wealth and apparent stability to the country, disaster for the Cuban family was brewing in our midst.

Government security must have been all over the place, but unseen by me. Both General Batista, the country's president, and Fidel Castro, about to overthrow him, used arguments in support of their actions and views on the way to best rule Cuba. Depending on what side you were on, you'd think and speak your feelings accordingly in support of one ideology or the other.

Under Batista, we enjoyed the immense benefit of a free press, except for the last two years of his mandate, 1957 and 1958 when he established Marshall law. It was all politics, a topic not frequently discussed with children. I didn't know any of this was going on, too young to be interested in government policies, and therefore totally absent from political discourse regarding military warfare about to destroy the world I---as well as the rest of the country---knew. My worries were a lot more mundane: What is Mom fixing for lunch? What will be waiting for me on Three Kings Day? When can I ride my Zundapp again?

Exactly one year before, on December 26, 1957, I was on my way to Barlovento when it happened. A question I frequently asked myself, after a near-death experience: Why was I spared? Shortly after leaving my Biltmore home on my Zundapp, I suddenly remembered having forgotten something back home. I made a sharp U-turn without looking back to see if anyone was coming. A man driving a VW Beetle was close enough to my tail, unable to miss running into me, touched my front wheel as he violently attempted to avoid me by turning to his left.

My motorcycle and I spun a few times around while he drove straight into a light post. Shortly after that, as I woke up from a mild concussion, my hands and elbows with superficial scrapes and abrasions, I opened my eyes to see a blurred vision of this man's face bleeding from a hole in his forehead.

My guardian angel was there that day. I don't recall asking Mother about the man's fate, probably too scared to know, but I am certain my angel kept me safe, in that particular moment, at that particular place; that is how Mom explained it.

Now, December 1958 in Rita's home, I remember thinking about the accident when, looking around Rita's living room, I spotted my cousin Chachi.

I watched his mother, my aunt Ofelia, and Abuela Rita, help him up onto a chair where he proceeded to recite, from memory, in French, something previously prepared as a farewell to the year's end. He was a couple of years younger than me, and to me, he looked ridiculously nerdy, in his plaid shorts, standing on that chair. I loved Chachi very much, but there always seemed to be something that made it difficult for us to interact directly. I guess his lifestyle priorities were different from mine.

Orlando--- *Humberto, mira a Chachi. Tía Ofelia lo vistió para darnos la bienvenida.* (Humberto, look at Chachi. Aunt Ofelia dressed him up to render a welcome speech.)

Mayrita, as we all called her, and thankfully still do, was my favored cousin. She enjoyed holding my ear with her left hand while sucking her thumb with the right. Thus, everyone thought she was left-handed, like her father, Salvador, and was called "la

Zurdita" (Lefty). Such behavior drove Freudian sexual attraction, but Freud had nothing to do with the fact that we enjoyed each other's company. Another favored cousin, Silvia Almeyda, now deceased, may she rest in peace, was not present at the party. She was in Georgia, with her parents, Olivia (Avin) Piedra and Dr. David Almeyda, where David trained as an anesthesiologist.

Shortly before midnight, we all gathered to fulfill a Cuban New Year's tradition said to wash away all of the previous year's difficulties. Each member of the family, even the children, helped to fill a bucket with water and empty it vigorously out the front door. Many saw this tradition as witchcraft, but also knew it served the psychological purpose of uplifting the animus of those disheartened by failure. It helped sustain hope and trigger aspirations, in the belief they could address concerns with confidence and resolve.

Having washed away our sorrows from the previous year, we were ready to encourage good luck for the coming one. Exactly at midnight, following Spanish conventional belief, we each ate twelve grapes, one for each month of the year, on each stroke of the clock. As I held each grape in hand, with open mouth, I tried my best to make a meaningful wish---for good luck, prosperity, and happiness for everyone I loved, not an easy task to achieve. I clearly recall that moment, having difficulty swallowing the grapes in the correct manner while laughing at this craziness, knowing I could not finish them in time.

A few minutes after midnight, my uncle Orlando, his three-car security guard detail waiting outside, arrived at his mother Rita's house. I peeked out the window, knowing the mysteriously powerful men protecting my uncle's life were just a few feet away, leaning on the black-and-white *perseguidoras* (police cars) with the lights off to go unnoticed. Without wasting a minute, Uncle Orlando signaled all the adults present into a separate room. It felt weird. They all came out shortly after that, maybe twenty minutes or so; their facial expression showed concern; the party ended abruptly, I had no idea why, and we went home. The ride for us was short, as we lived just a few blocks away from Rita's house.

Shortly after arrival at home, my only recollection places me upstairs, in my parents' bedroom, on my mother's bed. Black-and-white, dark, and artificially lit images of Mom moving from the bed to her closet appear whenever I search for that instant---she was gathering important personal items and documents she kept in the family safe located inside the closet. I wish I had a wand to touch her soul at the very time, a couple of hours past midnight, she broke her heart and drained her spirit. Being an anesthesiologist, I can now define my level of awareness at the time as "moderate sedation," i.e., easily arousable, but unable to grasp most nearby activity. Dad left home not long after our arrival from Rita's house---I learned later, to retrieve false passports, already stamped with awarded visas by a government official he knew who worked in the Cuban State Department.

My next recollection places me inside Mom's car, driving away from our home for the last time, then, through Havana, a city normally vibrant in nightlife, to be celebrating New Year's Eve with lights and music, dance, and fireworks, but sadly strange and empty, deathly, and scary, afraid to show up for the change in power taking place that day. My dogs were not with us. In my nightmares, I often see mirrors, moving images of plants and animals, screams and silence---barking diminished.

Orlando--- *Abuela, dónde están Goya y Rebert?* (Grandma, where are Goya and Rebert?)

Abuela Esperanza--- *Yo no sé, pero pronto vendrán.* (I do not know; they will come soon.) *No te preocupes, todo vá a salir bien* (Don't worry, everything is going to be all right.)

All was not well—as a matter of fact, all was bad, about to become worse. We were moving through a quiet and dark Havana at around 4 a.m. Years later, I would learn why it was 4 am, and not 3 am or 5 am. Landín had advised his siblings not to leave the island before that precise time, for 4 a.m. was the time set for the president's departure from Columbia, the military central command airport, to Santo Domingo. My eyes watery, I insisted.

Orlando--- Where is Goya? Where is Rebert?

Humberto--- *Cállate*! (Shut up!)

Mom--- Do not talk like that to your brother!

Humberto--- He doesn't stop!

Batista was leaving the country accompanied by the most prominent members of his government, including the Cabinet, Congress, Supreme Court, and highest-ranked members of both the police and the national armed forces. Years later, during family outings, I heard that three days before New Year's day, my youngest uncle, Osvaldo (Chirrino) Piedra copiloted the airplane that flew Batista's family to New York City. Chirrino was shot down by Castro's T-33 vintage trainers aircraft two and a half years later at the failed Bay of Pigs invasion.

Dad's Ghost--- The president's entourage would remain in the Dominican Republic for approximately one year under security guarantee provided by Dominican dictator Rafael Leónidas Trujillo Molina for a purported amount of ten million US dollars. The US government denied Batista entry to the United States. After the year passed, Batista and his family moved first to Madeira, Portugal, and then to Madrid, Spain. He died fourteen years later, of a heart attack, on August 6, 1973, in Guadalmina, Málaga, on Spain's southern coast.

* * * * *

The night was silent in that early morning, the first day of 1959. I must have fallen asleep. I cannot imagine the stress my parents and Abuela Esperanza must have felt in their hearts and minds, sensing guerrillas closing in; not enough time for the ferry to save us. The ferry was scheduled to depart Havana for Key West at 10 a.m. on its first voyage since the preceding summer when an Executive Order canceled service, for security reasons, from its usual cruise schedule between Key West and Havana. American tourists had stopped coming to Havana in late 1957 to protect their safety, as advised by the US State Department.

As a high-ranking official in the government, my father was well versed in military intelligence and national security protocols. He was advised to seek our exodus using this route, as opposed to Havana's International Airport, Aeropuerto de Rancho Boyeros, located fifteen kilometers (nine miles) southwest of Havana. Rancho Boyeros was the first exit shut down by the guerrillas. Dad had been CEO of that facility, familiar with landing, takeoff, shelter, supply, and repair of aircraft, receiving and discharging passengers and cargo.

The sun woke me up just past 6 a.m. that first morning of 1959. It was hot, but most discomfort came from its bright light crashing through the car window. It's beyond extraordinary, as to seem impossible, to attempt an understanding of my parent's considerations of the situation at hand. Dozens of wild conclusions must have been reached through fearfully discerning every horrid possibility, as they pondered in anticipation of the dock entry gates opening. Three hours of agony and extreme anguish followed.

Many outrageous questions, but only one frequently recurring: "How close are the guerrillas?" "Awfully close, so we better hurry," was always the answer. Who would be the marplot to save us? How will this mental agony end? The car stayed increasingly hot. Working hard to appear decorous, Mom remained quiet; no time for discourse, as her thinking mind presented more questions than answers, certainly not one to be aired to the rest of us.

We were at the dock waiting in our cars to board the ferry "to freedom." We had lost Cuba, and with it, everything that mattered to that day suddenly became meaningless, as we struggled to survive. Never having experienced a challenge like this before, I was clueless about events my parents had feared in the past. Little did I know, a few hours later, during the ferry trip, our home would be ransacked by neighbors, "friends," and total strangers who learned, through radio and television news, we had left the country for good. Our personal life, my belongings, in one instant, like a tornado---worse because it was carried out on purpose by humans filled with envy and anger, looking for revenge---would be gone.

If I were to put music to that day, I would choose one song, "El Reloj" was a bolero hit in the '50s written by Mexican composer Alberto Cantoral and sung by Chilean heartthrob Lucho Gatica. The lyrics speak of a tragic moment in time, a clock ticking mercilessly toward a dire destiny. That was Cuba.

To our misfortune, lives lived were about to be left behind for good: Their last bolero was not danced.

Chapter 18

We Board the Ferry to Freedom

Cuba ferry service: watch the last trip from Havana to Florida in the 1960s | World news | The Guardian

To tell my story, I am mostly relying on explicit memory, the conscious, intentional recollection of information, previous experiences, and concepts attached to specific life-events. These are memories of events that happened to me directly or around me. Recollection of a battle for territory to accommodate my family's settlement was no longer one for Cuba, but a "battle for Miami." We had just lost our island paradise; there was not going to be another day ever again that felt and looked like all the previous days in the lives of everyone in those cars and on the ship. My family's breakdown from its traditional infrastructure began that day, and changed through the years, impacted by new circumstances of new lives, themselves touched by experiences of their own.

We began boarding the ferry around 1 p.m. The fare was $13.50 one way, or $26.00 round-trip. Back when the US and Cuba were friends, the *Liberian S.S. City of Havana* left Key West for Havana on Tuesdays, returning on Thursdays, and back to Havana on Fridays or Saturdays at 11:00 a.m. The voyage began again with a trip to Key West early morning Monday. The ship could accommodate five hundred passengers and one hundred and twenty-five cars, but that first day of 1959, a Thursday, only 50 passengers would board, to navigate ninety miles over seven hours.

Things were not exactly friendly in Havana. Just six months before, street and nightclub violence provoked fear among American tourists, leading the US State Department to advise US citizens against traveling to Cuba. Shortly thereafter, by presidential decree signed in August, Batista ordered the ferry service to stop immediately, unwise for the economy, an extraordinary case of necessity and urgency, but a better option than falling victim to bad press.

Batista had made January 1, 1959, the day for renewal of the ferry service, purportedly intended to recharge the economy. Tourist travel between Havana and Key West made up a significant portion of the island's revenue. Or was this, instead, a coincidence, or a true miracle? Had he planned it all along, knowing to provide multiple exit gates and opportunities to leave the island on this day, the last one of his mandate? When the gates opened, Dad drove his car into the parking area, followed by Mom and other family vehicles with mostly women and children. I have told the following story of our escape time and again.

We parked a short walk to the Port Authority's Immigration Office to check passports, purchase tickets, secure tourist visas, and obtain a ferried car parking spot hurriedly assigned. There were no cabins for passengers to nap or use privately for necessities. Everyone had open seating. Something was not right. The 10 a.m. departure time came and went, and we were still in the car. We were not comfortable. The other half dozen vehicles, mostly belonging to my family members, were all driven by my aunts and carrying my cousins.

The entire journey seemed creepy to me but somewhat adventurous. As in the 1971 hit song "American Pie," about the loss of innocence of the early rock-and-roll generation, this was to be the day *my* music died.

I continued,

We were waiting for Dad to come out of the Dockmaster Building when he suddenly appeared, alone. He walked hurriedly to the car, opened the trunk, pulled out an M1 Garand repeater rifle---a standard US service rifle during World War II and the Korean War: Dad always carried one in the trunk of the car—and headed back to the building. Shortly after that, several men exited the building and started waving their hands above their heads, directing us to drive the cars onto the ferry, which we did. Dad followed, shouting for us to board the ferry.

Dad--- *Vámos Chonita, Ofelia, Osilia, todos adentro de los carros. ¡Hay que abordar ahora mismo!* (C'mon Chonita, Ofelia, Osilia, all of you get in the cars. We must all board now!)

The cars were driven into the boat and securely parked. We all took the stairs to the second or third level and entered a large room with tables and chairs, what appeared to be the dining room. The vessel departed within thirty minutes, bringing us all to safety.

From this point, I would occasionally add:

Just after push-off from the pier, we heard gunfire from afar. One bullet broke a window in the ship's dining room where we were all sitting at a table when Abuela Esperanza started vomiting her breakfast.

Mom yelled, "Aléjense de la ventana" (get away from the window!), and we all hid under the tables, cagados en los pantalones (with shit in our pants) scared stiff. Mom screamed, "tírense al piso y escóndanse debajo de la mesa!" (get down to the floor and take cover under the table!) the guerrillas at port were firing rounds toward the ship

Wow! My listeners would exclaim as I dramatized the "facts" with ever-greater gusto and emotion.

Forty-two years (my father's lifetime) later, while living in Miami, Florida, my wife, and I invited an old friend, Ramón Quintero, to lunch at an Argentinian steakhouse, Las Vacas Gordas (The Fat Cows) on Miami Beach's Seventy-second Street. Quintero suffered from myasthenia gravis, a debilitating neuromuscular disease that limited his ambulation. Using a walker, he slowly made it across the street to the restaurant. Shortly after sitting down, he looked at me and asked,

"Sábes cómo tú y tu familia salieron de Cuba?" (Do you know how you and your family made it out of Cuba?)

Ramón had been a close friend from Cuba and business partner of my dad while living in Spain in the mid-'60s; they knew each other well. I answered, *"Sí, por supuesto"* (Yes, of course) and proceeded to tell my story, with all the scrutiny and emotion. He stopped me and said, *"No, así no es como sucedió."* (No, that is not how it happened.) I was not prepared for what I was about to hear.

* * * * *

The true story, as told by Ramón Quintero:

Ramón Quintero--- *Tu padre, mientras trabajaba en la aduana en La Habana, encargado de regular y facilitar el comercio internacional, de cobrar derechos de importación y de hacer cumplir las regulaciones estadounidenses, incluidos el comercio, las aduanas y la inmigración, se reunió con un capitán de buques comerciales que tenía un cargamento de bicicletas para descargar en el puerto. Su barco estaba atracado, pero carecía del dinero para cubrir los impuestos sobre los derechos de importación. Como Comisionado Adjunto a cargo de mercancías y personas que ingresan al país, tu padre sólo respondió al Comisario que aparentemente, respondiendo a una llamada de un empleado, ordenó al barco que pagara las tasas o regresara al puerto de salida original.* (Your dad, while working at customs in Havana, charged with regulating and facilitating international trade, collecting import duties, and enforcing US regulations, including trade, customs, and immigration, met a commercial vessel captain who had a shipment of bicycles to unload at the harbor. His ship was docked but lacked the money to cover import duty taxes. As deputy commissioner in charge of goods and people entering the country, your dad answered only to the commissioner, who apparently, answering a call from a clerk, ordered the ship to either pay the fees or go back to the original port of departure.)

He went on,

Ramón Quintero--- *Tu padre se negó a permitir que se llevara a cabo este castigo y se ofreció a pagar los impuestos de su bolsillo, salvando al capitán un gran daño irreparable. Felizmente, y sorprendentemente coincidente, que el Capitán fuera el encargado* *ese Día de Año Nuevo de pilotar el Ferry que te llevaría a la libertad. Al escuchar la difícil situación de Humberto y pedir ayuda, vino a devolver el favor.* (Your dad refused to allow this punishment to be carried out and offered to pay the taxes out of his pocket, saving the captain major irreparable damage. Happily, and amazingly coincidental, that captain was the one charged that New Year's Day with piloting the ferry that would take you to freedom. Upon hearing Humberto's plight and begging for help, he came in to pay back the favor.)

For months following dinner with Ramón, Mary Carmen and I would make light of my drama. We laughed and poked each other, knowing we could, not the case when I shared my most important moment in time, when my music died, the most relevant day in my life, with friends and peers. The former, was shared with love, the latter, with pain, subconsciously hiding many truths---from myself and others. Memories retained by me, that day, were blocked and temporarily shifted to "storage failure," not kept vivid as working memory. Fear and pain may have been cause for my fantasy ideation, dreaming what I wished to be true. I honestly think the guerrillas were there, but do not, with certainty, recall the horrifying noise of glass exploding nearby, nor bullets flying over our heads, nor ducking under tables.

* * * * *

The ferry arrived at Key West around 7 p.m. The voyage was calm, docking and disembarkation went smoothly, as US Customs and then Immigration and Naturalization Service personnel checked our documents and belongings. Our arrival to US soil was different from what it had ever been. There were government officials carefully checking us out, making sure we were not hiding anything. It felt a lot worse than weird, as if we were not welcome. The port authorities were legally bound by State Department guidelines to provide adequate facilities to shelter the repatriates and political exiles arriving unannounced. This arrival didn't feel the same as all others in the past, and that's because it wasn't.

This time, we were hiding a weapon inside my pillow. This time, there were a few dozen political Cuban exiles waiting outside, and Superboy was sitting on a gun hidden inside a seat cushion. Cuban citizens deported or voluntarily exiled from Batista's government traveled to Key West in protest to our arrival. Those waiting outside had heard a rumor that Landín was aboard the ferry, so they became a loud mob demanding his release to them while screaming words in Spanish I had never heard.

Esbirro: A faithful follower or political supporter, especially one prepared to engage in crime or dishonest practices by way of service---"the dictator's henchman."

Latifundistas: Rich landowners who had expulsed farmers from their farms and the poor from their homes---"protectors of illegal land ownership in Cuba."

Paredón: Standing rock wall behind those executed by a firing squad. The mob yelled: *"Pónlo contra la pared y dispárale!"* ("Put him up against the wall and shoot him!")

What were they complaining about? I thought we had been an example of virtue, and now we were accused of all these brutalities! Up to that fateful night, my deepest conviction was that all men and women were basically good, i.e., humanity equated goodwill. Beyond that night, my faith in people, and even in things, my perceptions of all behaviors and intentions became suspect. I stopped believing in humankind; I began to share my journey with those depressed humans who walk the dark road of gloom, a sad and miserable melancholy that triggers self-doubt, ending in a feeling of dejection and anger. It creeps up daily, like dirt from a mountain coming down to flood a village. I had lost my innocence.

Dad started distracting us with small talk. My parents did everything they could to keep us safe and insulated from the moment's reality, sharing information on a need-to-know basis. We got into our cars and started driving north on US 1 to Miami, the destiny city for most Cubans for political reasons on the darkest major road in the country, the Florida Keys Highway.

My parents and Abuela Esperanza were not talking, except for Dad, appropriately sustaining his teenagers' innocence.

Dad--- *Tú sabes, mi hijo* (You know, my son), *éste país no es extraño para nosotros* (this country is no stranger to us.) *¿Recuerdas cuando visitamos Miami Beach un par de veces contigo y tu hermano alojándonos en el Hotel Roney Plaza en Collins Avenue y la calle 23?* (Remember when we visited Miami Beach a few times with you and your brother staying at the Roney Plaza Hotel on Collins Avenue and 23rd Street?)

Mother was silent, hiding sobs of defeat and loss of a life she would never again experience, her worst moment in time. Dad seemed Ok. She was petrified.

Chapter 19

The Early Castro Era: Los Milicianos

Los Milicianos

These guys wanted to kill us.

"A revolution is not a dinner party, or writing an essay, or painting a picture, or doing embroidery. It cannot be so refined, so leisurely, and gentle, so temperate, kind, courteous, restrained, and magnanimous. A revolution is an insurrection, an act of violence by which one class overthrows another."
-- Mao Zedong

All revolutionary leaders are considered by most historians as having a common personality trait. They are all "collective narcissists," imbued with ideals of greatness, and filled with certainty of owning a God-given mission to free millions from injustice. Characterized by leading all members of a group, both they and the group enjoy an inflated view of their relationship with themselves, and others; it always requires external validation. Fidel Castro was such a leader.

Los Milicianos, the name given to those who fought the Revolution in the mountains of Cuba, were originally *campesinos* (tenant farmers and farmworkers), mostly uneducated, but others were urban laborers, employed in diverse businesses in cities throughout the country. Some were university students. They arrived at Havana on tanks and trucks, sporting battle attire, hanging rifles from the shoulder, or holding them in hand with raised arms, camouflage uniforms, dirty and dripping sweat, and an exceptionally large beard---"Los Barbudos" (The Bearded Ones). Leading a *caravana* (caravan) through central Cuba, cheered by hundreds of thousands of people lining the streets and sidewalks and filled with awe and wonder, a Victory Parade: an amazing spectacle, it commanded profound respect and veneration, as the crowd offered absolute support to Fidel, the new supreme leader.

From the dark predawn hours of first day of 1959, through to the summer of the year, the Castro Revolution began the year with the murder of hundreds and then thousands of Batista supporters. Many victims were *non-Batistianos* who approved of the status quo; they were perceived by others as supporters of the Batista regime simply because they were more successful than their critics. Many innocent victims were accused of being spies and informers, as acquaintances accusingly pointed their fingers at them. Some were shot on the spot; some were taken to their final destination by an angry/joyful mob. The victims, Cuban citizens whose only crime was opposition to the ruthless communist leaders, Fidel Castro, and Raul Castro, were beaten and mocked. True Batistianos were quickly "judged" and killed by firing squad, or paredón, then thrown into pits dug near Santiago de Cuba, Havana, and hundreds of towns throughout the island. Thankfully, I was not witness to this tragic human behavior. It was the beginning of our national exodus; sixty years strong, and still going.

The first thing Castro did, besides keeping a Cuban "Habano" cigar in his mouth, upon gaining power, was expropriate most private businesses and privately owned property---including US holdings---and belongings of those leaving or about to leave the country, immediately losing their jobs when they announced their intention to leave. Tagged as traitors of the Revolution, they quickly became persona-non-grata to all who knew them. From that moment, their family, and friends, were watched closely for signs of antirevolutionary behavior.

Comités de Barrios, (Neighborhood Committees for the Defense of the Revolution, CDR) began to form. These "chivato" (informer) groups were instructed to observe and report every suspicious comment or action of neighbors, friends, and family, becoming the eyes and ears of the government. Diversity of opinion and envy became common triggers for deleterious behavior, rating-out those who, only recently, had been exalted and adulated. Established on September 28, 1960, they became a feared but necessary government institution---tangible asset for inspection and administration of citizens' control methods---with a slogan: *"En cada barrio, Revolución"* ("In every neighborhood, Revolution.") The CDR was also assigned, among other things, the responsibility to keep the neighborhood clean and organized, a task intended to facilitate the gathering of "national security" information and assemble the people to ride buses to and from Fidel's rallies to "voluntarily" listen and applaud propaganda speeches lasting hours on end.

Castro had effectively---to guaranty the system's subsistence--- converted the Cuban population into mosquitoes: some, deemed harmful enough to spread viruses like West Nile, dengue, and Zika---counter revolutionary behaviors that could lead to his government's demise---while others, became a nuisance, who bite people without spreading danger and system disruption of the new order. The regime would now control all basic needs, including food, visitors, conversations, material purchases, residential habitats, and professional activities. Cameras were installed in every corner for citizen surveillance.

Then, more than ever before, the human larvae---the Cuban people---became the victims of all members of an intelligence organization led by the Castro brothers, who personally directed the activities of each and all citizen as if they were enemies of the Revolution---guilty before proven innocent---a self-inflicted punishment that penalized their own people who, over the years, became their worst enemies.

In 1961, he declared: "Cuban children are property of the government." The "Operation Peter Pan," was a clandestine mass exodus of over 14,000 unaccompanied Cuban minors, ages six to eighteen, to the United States over a two-year span from 1960 to 1962, organized by Father Bryan O. Walsh, of the Catholic

Welfare Bureau. The children were sent out of the country by their parents who were alarmed by the rumors circulating amongst Cuban families that the new government, under Fidel Castro, was planning to terminate parental rights, and place minors in communist indoctrination centers. The operation was the largest mass exodus of minor refugees in the Western Hemisphere at the time.

Batista was no angel. Many Cuban exiles believe that he was cause and effect of our horrible destiny. I have heard dozens of personal friends, neighbors, coworkers, and strangers opine that "there would be no Castro if not for Batista." I agree with that, to some degree, and accept responsibility on behalf of my family. As a child and later as adult, I witnessed multiple undesirable consequences from Batista's unfortunate actions that, now, I directly attribute to misguided policies emanating from his government.

On arrival to the United States on the first day of the year 1959, I did not know that my home was being ransacked by neighbors, friends, and others. It was hard to see with owl's eyes, and no one appeared to be an eagle, but everyone around me persevered, worked hard, provided safety and comfort, induced, and supported progress, and tried, successfully for the most part, to strengthen Christian values. The new environment demanded changes, and the road to success defined assimilation. "When in Rome, act like a Roman." I felt protected and safe, exempt from fear as we approached a new beginning.

After the Garcias and Piedras migrated to the United States, we experienced specific contortions of both public and private lives, accepting odd jobs with low salary, survival work needed for food on the table and roof overhead. Many professionals and well-to-do people worked in hotels as elevator operators, beach boys, valet parking drivers, factory line workers, babysitters, and maids, cleaning houses belonging to others.

Landín remained a loyal political ally of Batista, showing up for political exiles---mostly anti-Castro operatives---through actions, awareness, and empathy while providing financial sustenance to Batista's supporters and their families. Most Cuban exiles continued to do the same---provide necessary help to some family and friends, inside as well as outside the island, through the next sixty-two years and one hundred and fifty days (twenty-two thousand seven hundred and eighty days, as of June 1, 2021).

Likewise, Dad's duty was accomplished, both in Miami---giving away food and household cleaning supplies at Jomares Market, his Wynwood grocery (1959 – 1963), and Madrid---politically maneuvering to get Cubans exiled in Madrid (1963 – 1967) to the US, their intended destination. Oscar Piedra, worked at the Port of Miami docks moving merchandise; Papi, cleaned homes and did construction work; Tito, worked as handyman at Jackson Memorial Hospital; and Tata, moved to Puerto Rico. Chirrino, joined the 2506 Brigade, or Democratic Revolutionary Front (DRF), giving his life for home and country. Of the five Piedra women, Ondina, studied at the college level, incorporating into the workforce as pharmacist (Jackson Memorial Hospital), and school counselor (Miami Senior High School), Ofelia, Olivia, Oraida, and Osilia, stayed home to care for the family household.

According to Jorge Duany, among some of the many challenges facing our "hybrid cultural identity" that maintains transnational linkages to the homeland as well as to the adopted country, the stereotyped images of the Cuban population in the United States' as well as other recent immigrants in the US and elsewhere's material success, have little basis on academic research's profile as "portraits" of the Cuban diaspora, and, should take into account its socioeconomic diversity, historical complexity, and physical dispersion.[4]

God--- So, Orlando, getting back to your childhood story. Your family was well connected. You and all its members enjoyed a high standard of living. Things went well for you until they didn't. Now, after the political rhetoric and recent Cuban history reviewed, begin to tell the truth about you. We've heard enough about Cuba.

Orlando --- It was tough for me.

EXILE
Part 5

---•---

American Teen

(1959 - 1962)

Chapter 20
Return to Graham Eckes School

Now that we were political exiles, our Three Kings Day gifts were different.

Humberto and I were no longer considered or perceived as higher class, from a privileged family. Now, victims of our "luxury trap," accustomed to special treatment and reverence, with daily access to our private club atmosphere and viewed as privileged children, we had sadly gained a need to own those privileges forever.

There were only six or seven Cuban-born students at Graham-Eckes: this allowed us to spend more of our time with American kids who did not speak Spanish. Although it offered an opportunity to strengthen spoken English skills learned in the previous four summer months at Culver, and the previous Fall semester at Graham Eckes, it also meant subjecting ourselves to occasional ridicule.

Sundays, the Spanish teacher, and his wife, would bring us and other Catholic children to mass in a yellow public-school bus, maybe to camouflage our rich-kid private-school status image, or maybe, they just rented it for lack of owning one.

The school's social curriculum included cotillions every Friday night, with a black-tie dinner followed by a gala dance. The boys sported a black tuxedo, and the girls, cocktail dresses.

Intended to teach students how to serve a formal dinner, in line with various and cultural traditions (as kept by the country of origin's teacher sitting at the head of the dinner table,) each student was assigned a specific table for a week. This tradition was attractive to me when I first read the school brochure, blind to the weirdest moment I would experience at Graham-Eckes, the most embarrassing day of my life, February 6, 1959.

Coincidentally, three days earlier, Tuesday, February 3 the *rock 'n rollers* Buddy Holly---*"Peggy Sue"* and *"That'll Be The Day"*, Ritchie Valens---*"Oh Donna"* and *"La Bamba"*, and J.P. Richardson aka The Big Bopper---*"Chantilly Lace"*--- were killed in a plane crash near Clear Lake, Iowa. That day has been immortalized as "the day the music died," a concept that has had much meaning in *my* life.

A cotillion was held on that first Friday of February 1959, a month and a week following our escape from Havana---the day *my* music died. I was assigned to the German teacher's table. I had often watched movies of Nazis murdering Jews during the Second World War, i.e., the Holocaust, so I was terrified. Each table offered seating for eight to ten people for dinner. First, you serve the teacher's spouse, then their guest (if there is one), followed by the teacher, and lastly, the students.

Everything went well with the first part of the three-course dinner. I did not screw up serving the hors-d'oeuvre. It was a cold salad. However, the main course was steak au poivre. According to famed French steak specialist Francis Marie, steak au poivre originated in the nineteenth century in the bistros of Normandy, where noted figures took their female companions for late suppers, and where pepper's purported aphrodisiac properties may have proved most useful. The French have gained a reputation for sexy.

As I recall, we were serving French style (service a la Francoise), where all the food (or at least several courses) is brought out simultaneously, in an impressive display of serving dishes. The diners put the food on their plates by themselves while the waiter holds the tray. Each dinner is served from the left side. I was nervous and mistakenly brought the steaks tray to the teacher's left side, instead of serving his wife first. He looked at me with a somewhat threatening demeanor and speaking with a German accent exclaimed: "Serve my wife first, please!"

I struggled my raspy voice to apologize for my mistake, as I began to approach her; she was sitting to his right. She was much younger than he, about eighteen years old, provocative, and stunningly beautiful dressed in white lace, with a deep-cut V neckline exposing large, luscious breasts. Her green eyes sensuously droopy, I couldn't keep my eyes off her inseam, as hard as I tried, forgetting exactly where I was supposed to go next. She was blonde. I was full of lust and desire. I was twelve.

Armed with supreme intentions, trying to do my absolute best to perform my duty correctly, I went around him rounding to my right while staring at her breasts, now in full view of her nipples from behind, I presented the tray from her right instead of her left.

This time my teacher was unforgiving, sternly stroking a closed fist on the table as he muttered "from the left," which immediately provoked panic in me.

I dropped all the steaks on her chest and belly, the sterling silver now-empty tray loudly hitting the floor; and ran away from the main building all the way across the highway to the boathouse near the inland waterway (*el lago*). I hid between two sailboats--- déjà vu my experience at Culver when wetting my pants---writhing with severe abdominal pain for about two hours until found by the staff and brought back to the main campus across the highway. I spent the rest of the night waiting for my parents to arrive from Miami.

Mom's Ghost--- The school called me to get permission for an appendectomy.

Orlando--- Yes, Mom, the diagnosis was given by the school nurse based on my really bad belly ache.

I did not have appendicitis, as diagnosed but a severe bout of colic due to uncontrolled stress and anxiety caused by the dinner incident.

Dad's Ghost--- Your mother and I drove from Miami that night, arrived at Palm Beach the next day, and returned home the day after.

For many, the teenage years are the best years of their life, but for some, they are the worst.

Orlando--- One can take on adult responsibilities, but still act like a child.

Humberto's Ghost--- That is your perception. How long did you expect to continue being irresponsibly childish?

For the next two or three weeks, I was mocked by students who had witnessed the fiasco. I thought the ridicule would never end, but it did.

* * * * *

As we left our teens and continued to adulthood, there were a few valuable lessons I learned from my difficult years while at Graham-Eckes School.

I learned that life is not fair. **Circumstances are driven by someone else's convenience.** At one of the formal galas, following a personal introduction by Dr. Graham herself---with instructions to be the young woman's guide and escort---I was offered an unexpected companion I could befriend and impress with topics familiar to me: motorcycle racing at Barlovento, boxing at Culver, sports at Miramar Yacht Club, and other activities that were foreign to her. Priscilla Allison, a millionaire Virginian who visited Palm Beach during winter season with her grandmother, herself a close friend of Dr. Graham, became my second crush. We shared only three Friday nights at the galas, where she wore a long evening dress adorned with jewels and a Pamela hat, very Palm Beach. After the fourth week, she and her grandmother returned to Virginia, and we never saw each other again. To me, a lost opportunity to lead a glamorous millionaire life supporting my habitual luxury trap, a false feeling since I did not belong in that world.

I also learned that **family matters more than friends.** Blood ties bind a sense of belonging. Familial love is reasonably stronger than friendship love. Most people do not realize the value of family and place more interest and faith in peers rather than parents. Understanding the difference between blood ties and sometimes fleeting relationships may save many from impending danger arriving in veiled forms.

Losing Priscilla was not particularly significant, as I quickly forgot she ever crossed my path. Her feelings were probably identical. More to the point, my two-faced Cuban "friends" proved fickle. Before Christmas break, we shared a cultural bond that shortened social barriers and allowed personal interactions to flourish. We were meaningful to each other for a while, then suddenly we were not. The rest of the year felt weird, as we became progressively isolated from the Hispanic group, once they learned we were no longer of the same social status.

I learned that **both family and friends treat you the way you treat yourself, not them.** As much as I could, I intuitively kept myself well. I don't believe I was always in control of what I did or thought, but I tried to take advantage of the perks offered at the school, and I noticed my interactions with other students improved over time. I saw those years as an opportunity to learn, show others who I was and would turn out to be---who and what I would become. I enjoyed all meals, especially breakfast---the twenty-four-fried-eggs tray that came to each table every morning, was mind-blowing. I frequently ate five or six out of the twenty-four with grits and bacon. I participated in all sports---karate, tennis, swimming, sailing and board games---my favorite was chess---and occasionally watching the stars through a potent telescope owned by a friend. He and I would set it up in the area of the tennis courts. I loved getting in touch with the universe. I felt loved and appreciated and know for certain others noticed the boy from Cuba not just surviving but also making friends and accomplishing goals.

Looking back to the past years, as elderly adults do, often brings a feeling of not having done enough toward achieving a better life later. I spent too much time lamenting my separation from Mom and Dad, my home and toys, my dogs and friends at Miramar Yacht Club and everything else I enjoyed in Havana.

I **knew the sacrifice would pay off,** so I studied hard and played hard as I looked to the future. After high school in Miami, we moved to Spain so Humberto and I could attend medical school, then, I practiced medicine in the US and raised a healthy family.

I learned that **things either don't matter that much, or they matter a lot, depending on personal circumstance.** Earthly possessions are raw materials that help you move from one place to another. I wanted "things" because I had heard I wanted them or needed them for my happiness. In contrast to a perceived need for things, I was sensitive to a homeless man sleeping at the entrance steps to the Catholic church I attended. Thinking how unfit to live, how sad and distraught this person looked, lacking essential things, adequate clothing, a car, a home to go to, and a family to support, strengthened my conviction that it is better to share whatever you own. With much less than I, he may have enjoyed the spirituality I lacked, not bothered by his social and strained economic status. I never detected envy or animosity in this man. I felt he was more independent than I had ever been. But I did not want to be him.

I learned that **morning follows even the longest night. God has a plan for you.** No matter how dark it looks right now, it will get better with time. Patience and Hope will make it happen. The many nights I spent alone looking at the ceiling while lying in bed, dreaming I would be home soon, turned out to be worse than the next day. Those starry nights, when we went out to the tennis courts to look at the galaxy and the planets through my friend's telescope, helped me understand the smallness of our existence and the power of the universe. It helped my animus and lifted my spirits.

I learned that **happiness is a choice, and it requires a lot of hard work.** I learned to look in the mirror and be thankful for my blessings. Insight is not something I got from others, but it is something I experienced from within. My reality was mostly in tune with my expectations, as I went about life at the school one day after another. I felt certain I did not belong. I was happy the day I left. I missed home and was unable to make significantly good enough acquaintances to desire to stay another year. But I spent most of my time there enjoying new challenges, acquaintances, and places we visited. Although achieving happiness is part of who I am, its presence is often circumstantial and contextual, triggered by our conscious decision to look at things in a bright light.

"Nothing will work unless you do."
--- Maya Angelou

And, finally, I learned that **time is our biggest asset.** When at last I learned this, I tried not to waste time worrying about the past or the future. I thought, "It is passing by the second, so grab it now." I never dreamed my time at the school would go so quickly. I felt fortunate to have lived experiences available to a privileged few. To live in the moment, or now, meant being conscious, aware, and in the present with all of my senses. I have to admit to getting into "down" moods each time I felt lonely, but I was never alone, nor had few opportunities for fun and games. I usually enjoyed my time whether solo or in someone's company. I was happy. I was coming home to Miami.

Chapter 21

Flamingo Park

Six months after arrival in the United States, my parents, my sister, and Abuela Esperanza lived in a rented apartment on Meridian Avenue and Dade Boulevard, in Miami Beach. Humberto and I were living at Graham-Eckes, in Palm Beach, two hours north from Miami. In the summer of 1959, Dad rented a house on Española Way and Meridian Avenue, shaded by canopied old oak trees that peacefully darkened each sidewalk and the boulevard. The house backed up to Flamingo Park, a huge sports facility offering sixteen clay tennis courts and an Olympic-size swimming pool.

We had arrived home.

Mom--- *Vamos niños, ya llegamos. Cojan sus cosas, y ayuden a su padre con el equipaje.* (C'mon kids, we are here. Get your things and help you father with the luggage.)
Orlando--- *Sí, Mamá.* (Yes, Mom.)
Humberto--- *No, Gallego, tú cuida a Ana María, yo me encargo de ayudar a Papá.* (No, Gallego, you take care of Ana Maria, and I will help Dad.)

Flamingo Park was a skip and a jump over the chain-link fence from our backyard easement. I was awestruck, filled with wonder, thankful for the opportunity to play and participate in competitive sports offered at the park. For the next year, our---Humberto's and mine---lives would be glued to the park. There would be no day or night when the park was absent from the list of possibilities when discussing the events of the day.

Ana Maria, three years old, remained at home with Abuela Esperanza and Mom, too young for kindergarten. She was the joy of the family. Mom occasionally brought her to the park and sometimes enjoyed the children's pool.

We enrolled in eighth grade at Eli Fischer Middle School, at 1424 Drexel Avenue, three blocks from our home. I was thirteen years old. In the meantime, Dad got busy looking at business opportunities.

Dad's Ghost--- *De nuevo, teníamos la libertad de perseguir un espíritu nacional fuera de Cuba, en los Estados Unidos, lo cual reflejó un conjunto de ideales --- democracia, derechos humanos, libertad personal, oportunidad de igualdad--- en los que la libertad pudo florecer.* (Again, we had the freedom to pursue a national ethos outside of Cuba, in the United States, which mirrored a set of ideals--- democracy, human rights, personal liberty, opportunity, and equality--- in which freedom flourished.) *De nuevo libres!* (Free again!)

As Dad recharged his batteries in support of upward social mobility for the family and children, Humberto and I remained aloofly exempted from feeling the squeeze of a tight budget. Both Mom and Dad polished their English skills as Mom kept tabs on Abuela Rita, her brothers, and her sisters. Landín was still in the Dominican Republic keeping an eye on the president. Tata moved to Puerto Rico with his wife and two children, and Osilia also moved there with her husband, Gustavo, and their children. Chirrino joined a secret CIA-backed anti-Castro military-mercenary group called Brigade 2506 and began training for the failed Bay of Pigs invasion of Cuba on April 17, 1961. His airplane would be shot down during the liberation effort. Abuela Rita, as well as the Piedra family, never forgave President John F. Kennedy for his cowardly abandonment of our Cuban patriots.

Mom got busy getting everyone settled.

It was challenging work in a strange society, charting my parents', uncles', aunts', and cousins' goals, hopes, and dreams.

The amazing Jewish community and their tax money paid for paradise. Back then, when my heart was pure and my mind was clean (to a degree), I had the privilege to partake in an amazing spiritual experience. Every evening at sundown, in the shade under a large oak and a huge orange-red flamboyant royal poinciana, next to the handball courts, a couple dozen elderly Eastern European Ashkenazi Jews gathered, occupying an area equivalent to approximately 1200 square feet.

They carried their own folded aluminum chairs from home to the park and back; the same chairs they used to sit at the beach to sunbathe every morning. They met to talk, in Yiddish, their traditional language, about the horrible experiences as Holocaust survivors, memorializing friends and family victims of the Third Reich. I did not then or now speak Yiddish, but saw their pain, heard their raspy voices, and imagined their grief. Those lovely people, wisdom-filled with a lot of character, on very tight budgets, with a million miles of hardship, now in the waiting room of Heaven, played a key role in what Miami Beach is today.

Their hope, as well as ours, for a better, more peaceful life became the objective to achieve. We had both made it, safe at last, free from criminality and murder.

To me, a know-nothing teenager trying to figure out my new world, it seemed they all suffered from some skin disease, a myriad of dry wrinkles surrounding lean old bodies. It was all related to chronic exposure to the sun for hours, day after day. Everyone living here today speaks Spanish, even more so than English.

I miss the old South Beach feel, and Yiddish remains in my memory and heart as a part of me. I do not see those old Jews anymore, but I can still hear and see them through my imagination when I visit Flamingo Park.

We played Little League baseball at the park. Little League teams were sponsored by local businesses: Pumpernik's, Rascal House, Wolfie's, Chris Dundee, and others. Skip Bertman---of LSU-fame---was the best baseball coach in the program. He also coached pony league.

Humberto and I would walk over in spikes to the baseball field, with our gloves and bats and a couple of balls, looking for friends to play with; not finding any, we would practice throwing and catching the ball together. During the season, we practiced daily, just like at Miramar Yacht Club.

It was beginning to feel like home again.

Chapter 22
Miami Beach Senior High School

In the summer of 1960, we moved from Española Way to 2395 North Meridian Avenue. It was a two-story Spanish Colonial on a double lot with a one-car garage. The entrance was a long, covered hallway leading to the front door. Two blocks away was the spanking-new Miami Beach Senior High School (MBSHS)---my parents always found a house in walking distance to school---located at the corner of Prairie Avenue and Dade Boulevard. It had just opened its doors to Miami Beach residents. We both registered in ninth grade. Ours, the Class of 1963, was the first freshman class to graduate. Living so close, Humberto and I walked to class every day.

The new facility presented a wonderful opportunity to make new friends, experience challenges never seen before, and blend in with American teens. My wish to be one of them recharged as I grew more independent. Some athletics practices were held on school grounds: football and basketball. Others were held at Flamingo Park: tennis, track and field, and swimming. Both Humberto and I became involved with almost every sport, but only he had the consistency of attending every practice. He lettered in several sports. I, in none.

A typical day at school started with the general information period lasting fifteen minutes. Then, everyone went to first class, then second, and so on, up to seven. Break periods were meant for socializing. A lot of tobacco smoking went on, but no drugs, including marijuana.

At that time, I suffered a severe case of acne, which impacted my self-image in a significant way. I lost my ability to look a girl or boy in the eye, turning my gaze away from them the second I felt they were looking at my face. Coexisting with other identity crises and romantic crushes, this poor self-image turned my life into a whirlwind of daily "mind-blowing" experiences.

I projected onto myself another person's idealized attributes, and admired values I wished to own. Those strong positive feelings to be liked and be like those other students identified as role models, played to the perfectly wonderful image I created.

This new attitude triggered new dreams and hopes having more to do with fantasy than with reality, telling much more about the admirer (me) than the admired (them). Because most fantasized feelings proved unrealistic, fading in a relatively short time, these crushes soon wore off and died. But the damage done by my exposed camouflage impinged my personality.

I suppose Mother knew and attempted to modulate my identity rollercoaster but failed. She sensed my transformation into someone I admired, wanted to become, or proved eager to imitate and follow. There was little she could do to prevent me from falling victim to generational changes brought about through peer pressure.

I was changing from the person I had been reared to be to the new "me," more akin to those I wanted to emulate. I was being "absorbed," assimilated and forever defined as any American kid, just as I dreamed.

We mixed well with other students in school. My friends were not the same as my brother's. My crowd was less aggressive and demanding, not as driven by schoolwide projects. Volunteer academic clubs for languages (Spanish was the largest), English, math, history, and government, plus other subjects in science and arts, competed for students' interest in social clubs and sports. I belonged to the Spanish club, the French club, and the Debate club.

Social groups began to form, some limited by financial status, others by sports participation, some seeking to belong at a higher social level where popularity prevailed as individual attributes were displayed and allowed to shine among the rest. Jocks hung out with beauty queens vying for cheerleader spots and sidekicks. Nerds stayed away from them, while gays mixed among both celebrities-to-be and studious types.

We went out a lot, dating someone we just met yesterday. Some, like myself, became attached early to one partner who eventually became our girlfriend or boyfriend. We partied at dances in public halls every Friday and Saturday night.

There were no black students at MBSHS for most of my time there. The school integrated in 1961-62, a year before my graduation. The first two African Americans, a descriptive term unused during the sixties, a boy and a girl behaved very proper and scared. There were ten billion reasons for them to be. But not being black, or brown, how was I supposed to be sensitive to the pain and distress from centuries of abuse suffered every single day by blacks in America?

I don't know about my brother, his feelings usually unclear regarding the topic of race, but I felt bewildered and concerned. How could a situation like this, obviously racist, exist in a liberal society leading the world in freedom, human rights, and democracy?

No vision presents enough transparency to accept the reality of two worlds. La Salle in Cuba and Beach High in the US were both segregated, and, today, I see that as not okay; not then, when I felt the opposite, with the caveat of cultural difference.

Historically, both countries took advantage of slavery—if you were white--- and abhorred it if you were black. Mulattos lived in Cuba, the Caribbean, and Brazil for the most part. There were a lot more mulattos in Cuba (thirty to fifty percent of the population) than in South Florida; not one in Miami Beach, unless employed by tourism.

Aha! Some Americans did not mix races, but instead bullied Mexicans, Central and South Americans, and immigrants from the Caribbean Islands, Africa, and Asia. Some Americans felt we were not equal to them, they were "superior." I wondered, why did I not see this before while at segregated Culver and Graham-Eckes?

This prejudiced attitude seemed new information, but it was not new to me. I had experienced that noninclusive social distancing in Cuba, both at school and at the yacht club. Maybe I was too young to tell.

On the other hand, many neighbors, teachers, young and old acquaintances, coaches, and strangers opened their hearts to us and insisted on helping us feel welcomed in the US. I picked up new buddies from mostly white Cuban and Jewish communities. Sports participation provided the outlet to switch focus from negatives to positives.

Boxing was the one sport I couldn't abandon while watching it on TV or at the Fifth Street gym. I only boxed competitively at Culver Military Academy Summer Camp and had a lot of fun doing it. I followed those contests closely, first watching the "Brown Bomber," Joe Louis, World Heavyweight Champion from 1937 to 1949, and then Rocky Marciano, the only heavyweight champion to have finished his career undefeated, holding the world heavyweight title from 1952 to 1956. Louis looked amazing on televised bouts from Madison Square Garden. Victorious in twenty-five consecutive title defenses, knocking down opponents with his signature left hook to the liver, the Bomber looked unbeatable.

However, "the Greatest," the "Most Beautiful," and the most impacting boxer at the time was Cassius Clay. That was his name when I met him at Reisler Bro. Sport Shop at 1671 Alton Road in Miami Beach during training for the 1960 Rome Olympics. While I was browsing sports merchandise on the shelves, Mr. Reisler encouraged me to "come out to meet the future Heavyweight Champion of the World." As I turned the corner at the end of the aisle, there he was, a tall, lanky black man, cocky and smiling, appearing too thin to win a heavyweight crown; but I didn't tell him, "so he wouldn't feel bad," when he extended his hand to shake mine---I smiled---disappointed.

Orlando--- Nice to meet you, Champ!
Clay--- Nice to meet you.

What an opportunity I missed to kiss his hands, the best fists the sports world has ever seen! We had already moved to Spain by the time he won the World Heavyweight crown from Sony Liston at the Miami Beach Convention Center on February 25, 1964. Clay won by technical knockout in the seventh round when Liston's corner held him back from fighting the round. He had broken Liston's arm and dislocated his shoulder with forty to fifty jabs hitting their target at the speed of light.

He became my new superhero.

Chapter 23

We Get Our Dogs Back

Humberto / Ana Maria with dogs / Orlando

How can I describe the indescribable? Miracles happen, people we have not seen in decades cross our paths unexpectedly, we hit the lotto or find the job of a lifetime. But the story I am about to tell you is simply amazing, unbelievable, and nothing less than miraculous.

One cannot argue the loyalty and dedication dogs show their owners. They are even known to become depressed and die due to the broken heart phenomenon, like an old couple who are together for most of their lives. A part of us dies when they die, like losing family. This deep feeling of losing a friend is what I experienced the night we left Havana, leaving our dogs behind.

Orlando--- Where is Goya?

No answer. Both, the Dalmatian female, who I named Goya and her brother Rebert were graciously gifted as puppies to my father by the Brazilian ambassador to Cuba, as a thankful gesture for a favor Dad once did for him. Unknowingly, I named her after the Spanish painter Francisco Goya—a male. Rebert was given a French name because it sounded "cool" but had no meaning. We often took them out for rides, went to the beach or a park. They loved to run. Rebert was meek, generous sized, slow, and clumsy. So good-natured and loving, especially with children, made him special.

Goya was smart, vigilant, thin, agile, and quick off the ground, possessed excellent endurance and stamina, always seeking the source of an unusual, atypical, or bizarre fragrance moving in her direction. She would stand very still in cervical spine extension, protruding snout above her ears. Friends, neighbors, and family who visited sensed her hostility, and rightly so. I don't recall her biting anyone in Cuba, but all she had to do was look at you to send a clear message: Don't come any closer.

Mom fed her and I bathed her; Luis (the chauffeur) took her for rides in Dad's black Cadillac Eldorado; and our chef, Modesto, occasionally sat on a patio chair in the back yard when she was there, but his fear kept him from petting her. The night we left Cuba for good, we opened a debt account. I know they missed us the moment the noise stopped as the cars with us in them drove off our driveway. When I asked for them, there was only silence. Not another word about my two dogs was uttered by either my grandmother, mother, or father for the next 26 months.

One stormy night in the winter of 1961, around eight o'clock, two years and two months after leaving Cuba, Mom asked me to accompany her to Burdines Department Store, known at the time for carrying high-end clothing and home décor items---a South Beach staple on Lincoln Road. Leaving our home on North Meridian Avenue, my mother drove her candy-apple red 1957 Plymouth station wagon south toward Lincoln Road. The store was closing at nine.

A tropical storm was brewing, and heavy rain was falling hard from pitch dark skies all around us, brutally spraying gushes of water on the roof of our car, with strong lateral gusts smashing onto the car windows. The surroundings were hardly visible, lit up by occasional lightning. Mom stopped at the traffic light on the corner of Meridian Avenue and Dade Boulevard when another car, also a station wagon heading in the same direction and driven by another woman, stopped to our right with intention to make a right turn at the light.

Mom looked straight ahead, turning her head toward the road and up slightly to the red light. Suddenly, I looked to my right again. As I turned my head in their direction, I spotted a dog in the back that was looking toward our car. It was a Dalmatian. Surprisingly, the dog started pacing front to back in this lady's car. It was really loud inside the car as tons of water drenched the windshield. It felt like a car wash. The front windows were left open a few inches to prevent windshield fogging,

Orlando--- Look, Mom, a Dalmatian!
Mom--- Yes, she's slender. What a beauty!
Orlando--- It's Goya!!!

Mom--- *No, mi hijito, Goya está muerta.* (No, my little boy, Goya is dead.)

Orlando--- You are lying! You never told me. Please, Mom, look at her, it's Goya.

As the light turned green, I turned my head in their direction one more time, observing this beautiful canine standing on four legs, again turning her head toward us as the car made a right turn to head west toward Miami. My mother, with tears in her eyes, slowly pushed on the gas pedal to go straight. I grabbed the steering wheel with force and determination, pleading with Mom to go right, follow the car, and make sure this was not Goya.

Orlando--- Mom! Follow that car! Turn right! It's Goya! It's Goya!

Mom--- Let it go, darling. That is not Goya. She died in Cuba.

Orlando--- You are lying!

Mom--- Orlando, please, please...

She pleaded with me.

She realized she had no choice. Superboy had a death grip on the steering wheel. He was not about to be denied, and she understood this well. She looked at me and made a right turn. We followed that lady's car for twenty-five or thirty minutes, seeing only her red taillights, to this woman's house.

She lived in Hialeah, a city located northwest of Miami where many Cubans moved to in the early years of political exile. Most of the city's residents were and are Cuban, so we assumed this woman was Cuban.

As she pulled into her driveway, we followed her in and stopped our car right behind hers. After a few seconds, wondering when she would exit her car, under heavy rain, she came out with a hairbrush in one hand and the dog on a leash in the other, and screamed at us in Spanish.

Woman--- *¡Aléjense de mí!"* (Stay away from me!). *Éste perro es una fiera* (This dog is a killer beast) *y los matará si se acercan!* (and will kill you if you get any closer!)

With no time left for her to say another word, and with no words coming from us, Goya barked once and leaped toward me, releasing herself from her temporary owner with the leash and all. The woman screamed, then stood silent, in awe, watching this amazing event with open mouth.

Mom did likewise with a smile, tears flowing so fast you couldn't tell them from the rain. Still pouring heavily, now on her driveway and front lawn, both the woman and Mom watched a boy and his dog reunite.

Woman--- *Ay, Dios mío!* (OMG!)

They must have been in shock seeing Goya licking my face--- in awe as the rain fell on us. There was total silence. God had just permitted us to reclaim a part of what we'd lost, both the dog and I on the mud next to the driveway.

All the pain disappeared, the loss of lifestyle, country, job, our house, assets, family life, and the dream of going back home. No need now because home came to us in Miami.

A Cuban mother two years after losing her base, bringing up her three children while serving the traditional role of immigrant wife to her husband in the land she now called "my country," all okay now in a moment of ecstasy and joy.

Mom stared silently, with incredulous eyes that saw a miracle in the making. Goya kept licking my face, my mouth, my ears, my hair and wiggled her tail forcefully, finally reunited with her family. The dog never forgot our smell, our voices, our love. Mother turned to the woman and asked:

Mom--- Where is the male?

The stunned woman responded,

Woman--- Inside the house.

Now she knew with certainty, now she understood that we were their parents, that we would not leave without them. She did not even try to contest my mother's words that followed:

Mom--- *Cuánto le debo?* (How much do I owe you?)
Woman--- *Doscientos dólares* (Two hundred dollars.)

She responded without hesitation.

Woman--- *Vuelvo enseguida* (I'll be right back).

The woman didn't hesitate. She went inside the house to fetch Rebert. I guess she had it clear that this was the last time she would see them or us. Mom took out her checkbook and wrote her a check in the amount requested, a current value equivalent of $1,700. We then left with the dogs.

I could never thank both my mother and that woman enough for their kindness in allowing us to be reunited. We got both dogs in the back of the station wagon and drove off. Rebert knew that he was back with his family, but he wasn't as excited; with a more reserved personality he just kept looking at us, not speaking a word, probably resentful for being abandoned at our departure, but we knew what he was thinking. We knew what he would have said: "Thank you, God."

Unfortunately, three years later, the family moved to Spain and, again, left Goya and Rebert behind. This time, it was not an emergency departure; more like an urgency for Mom to find another place, a better place to continue the amazing labor of every woman who decides to give her life for others. But this time, this moment in time, would signify the last time, truly, the last time I would see my dogs.

Hundreds of stories span five wonderful years in South Beach, my new paradise, as Humberto and I ran around, got in heaps of trouble, and learned to adapt.

Around our home, most of the neighbors' backyards grew avocado trees. Beautiful and forgiving as they are, we climbed them to reach the fruits and sell them to the local Epicurean market or Dad's Jomares Market in Wynwood. Incredibly coincident, our youngest son, Javier (Javi) is general manager of a multi-venue food and beverage establishment located *exactly* on the property, *twenty fourth street and N, Miami Avenue,* where Dad owned and ran his grocery store, Jomares Market.

We studied at the best high school in Miami, went to the beach several times per week, worked as beach boys and valet at some hotels near Lincoln Road, attended dances and parties, high school football, basketball, baseball, and other team sports games... In some, we enjoyed a fabulous and amazing teen experience, but nothing compared to getting our dogs back.

And so it went, the most incredible dog story I know, now finally written.

Chapter 24

Puppy Love

Adolescence was a real challenge for me. I was voted president of the American Association of Sex Without a Partner. I know how bad that sounds; it was worse. My life was meaningless unless I was lusting after any two-legged human belonging to the female gender. I was the pitiful result of an insecure kid who saw himself as too short, ugly, weak, and limited by his insecurity. My fear was real. My acne did not improve with masturbation. My nickname, "Pizza Face," stuck in the midbrain like wet gum.

There was nothing wrong with sex, but much more sociologically profound and urgent for me at the time was my need to be one of *them*, to participate and integrate fully into "their" world, to share a life experience with those I admired— young, restless, nature-driven, environmentally authentic American teens—and to be accepted. I just wanted to feel that I belonged. Nevertheless, I was suspect about the wisdom of many customs and cultural tendencies they practiced in their daily lives.

Not a boring teenager, I socialized and participated in school activities. I even joined a fraternity. But I was not happy. Something vital to my mental health was missing, and it was not sex. I took a job as beach boy at one of the hotels on Collins Avenue near Lincoln Road. Besides providing pocket change, it made me feel useful while keeping fit and suntanned. All I needed was to feel part of the American Teenage Scene in which I prayed to quietly "dissolve" into a homogeneous mixture composed of me as the solute, the high school kids I admired, the solvent.

Girls were something to look at, but my feelings went beyond fear to terror. Intimidation and panic to potential cowardly abstractions kept me hidden and isolated. My hormones were coming and going uncontrolled. New romantic crushes formed and shortly solidified whenever I found someone who appeared powerfully attractive, with whom I felt excited to be around and wanted to spend a lot of time with. I was shy to begin dating, until the summer of 1960, when I met Madeline. I first spotted her at a dance at Ocean Drive and tenth Street in South Beach. She embodied everything I, a hot-blooded Latin teenager in a liberal society, needed: *Sex*. Her presence was stimulating, hormone-energizing, and lusciously appealing to me.

When standing near me while talking to her friends or walking, lightly dressed in shorts with a waistline three inches below the belly button, she was hot. Lust! Here we go again. Superboy was unconsciously looking for trouble, and he almost found it. Me and Madeline became friends, then lovers, and finally separated by destiny. It was a struggle, to say the least, as attempts at integrating her into our family failed time and again.

Humberto's Ghost--- Gallego, you drove me insane.

Mom's Ghost--- I prayed Madeline would not get pregnant. I would never agree to abortion. You were too young. We had too many problems. Your brother saved your hide many times.

God--- *Éramos veinte y parió Catana*. (We were twenty and *Catana* delivered)---almost!---an old Cuban saying implying really bad luck.

We were in a "puppy love" relationship for the better part of high school. She was of a split-religion family, her mother Jewish, and her father Catholic. She had a younger brother we called Nature Boy (nicknamed by my mother) and Little Tarzan (nicknamed by me) because of his physical ability to climb avocado and palm trees. He was always barefoot, shirtless, in swim trunks, and his light blond straight hair was long, naturally hanging straight down from his head, over and around his ears to his shoulders.

I gave Madeline enormous power of approval. My feelings of love—erotic desire—was overshadowed by a wish to be one of "them," respected, and appreciated. Wanting to be a "typical American" among fellow students at school, I was willing to do whatever it took to get into her good graces (and her pants), to encourage her to feel safe and natural around me. I went out of my way to be like her friends.

Encouraged by her as an accomplice, I created a *codependent attachment.* Totally engulfed in our teen fantasies, we behaved irresponsibly during those wild and crazy nights. Similar to the emotional bond that typically forms between infant and caregiver, by which the helpless infant gets primary needs met, her proximity and acquaintance became my engine for subsequent social, emotional, and cognitive development.

I fell victim to another individual's awareness--- interpretation of who I was and how I acted or behaved. I needed Superboy to step up. He guided me through fog and fire, holding my hand as only he could, while caressing my spirit and smoothing my fear.

Superboy--- You know there is pain and suffering from falling short of expectations. Your friends at school, the ones you felt needed your undivided attention, were not looking for you to become someone else other than yourself. You should have gone on with your life happy and content with whom you were.

I "had to be" spectacular to fit the persona others expected me to be. Building Superboy, I paid particular attention to all facets of *their* environment, and the thoughts in *their* heads. Important things, behaviors, and mores that I mirrored, as I ignored the rest, likely helped me, as with the original humans, to survive and evolve young Orlando into adulthood. It's a skill that can help children and adults alike succeed in school, at work, and in their relationships, sometimes at the expense of losing part of one's self-identity, losing myself in the process of becoming someone else.

I longed to be an American teenager and equated being a Jew to *having things* to achieve a higher status and to buy more things. Miami Beach's Jewish population was in charge of the city, and their wealth showed throughout tourist venues but especially in my neighborhood.

I dreamed of owning my own car, a new Vespa scooter—common transport in South Beach—dating a prettier girl, going to better restaurants, and buying fashionable clothing at boutique stores on Lincoln Road, made with the best cloth and tailored body-tight to look better and feel better. With more things, I could travel to more places, see "the world," see how others lived and study their culture to discover how they became powerful, what they did to have all the things they had. Having more things meant I would be happier. I tried to think like *them.*

It was pitiful.

This transitional period to adulthood brought up issues of independence and self-identity; I faced tough choices regarding school, sexuality, and alcohol available through social life. Pressure from peer groups, romantic interests, and "fashionable" personal appearance increased substantially over time.

Orlando--- *Mamá, ésta es Madeline.* (Mom, this is Madeline.)---I had brought her home to "meet my mother."
Mom--- *Madeline?*
Orlando--- *Sí, es mi novia.* (Yes, she's, my girlfriend.)
Mom--- *Tu qué?* (Your what?)

Mother knew perfectly well who Madeline was. She probably also knew of my intention to bring our relationship to a more formal stage, integrating my friends into my traditional Cuban Catholic family. But sadly, unprepared as we were, Madeline did not dress for the occasion.

Sporting tight mini shorts and a loose white blouse unbuttoned at the top and ending above her belly button, a pair of sneakers without socks, and no makeup, her unkept hair wildly messy, and no jewelry, Madeline was DOA (dead on arrival).

I should have known better. We were unpleasantly not welcomed. My youngest aunt and mother's closest confidant, Ondina, married to my uncle Orlando, was visiting at the time and overheard our conversation from the second floor. Ondina came down the stairs slowly approaching in a surveillant attitude, stopped at the middle of the stairway, and declared: "Who are you?"

Madeline remained silent, as I tried to ease what appeared as an increasingly distasteful confrontation. This being the first intimate encounter between our two cultures since my family had arrived as exiles to the United States, Madeline and I were about to lose the attempt at "integration." Many cultural divides presented a huge challenge to our life at that moment. Throughout childhood, and still as an adult, these challenges remain.

Shockingly, Ondina reached down for her shoe, aimed it at Madeline, and threw it in her direction. I can only imagine my poor girlfriend's shock and anguish. We left immediately, never to return as a couple, knowing another attempt would be as disastrous as the one just experienced. Both of us then became more isolated from my family culture, and I more distant from who I used to be, now fully embracing my new persona projected toward who I would become. But Madeline, traumatized by my family's rejection, wanted to break up. I talked her out of it.

As impacting as academics and sports were, sex-filled days and nights defined my high school years. In June 1962 I was sixteen and owned nineteen high school credits, enough to graduate. But everyone, including me, felt I was too young and immature for college. So, I voluntarily repeated my senior year, graduating in 1963 with twenty-five credits, six more than required for graduation; and still, seventeen. I stayed with Madeline for the entirety.

After three years of "going steady" with her, I moved with Humberto to Madrid, Spain, so we could begin premed at the Faculty of Medicine, University of Madrid. Humberto and I left Miami first, in early September 1963. Madeline stayed behind.

We wrote love letters every single day for almost a year, then twice a week across the Atlantic Ocean, increasingly less frequent and shorter than the previous one, as our relationship dwindled and extinguished by time and distance. Hampered by unforgiving and "impossible" odds against us, we became history at Christmas of 1965, the last letter from her, *the most disappointing day of my life.*

We did not see each other ever again.

Part 6

———————◆———————

I Get My Shit Together

(1963-1967)

Chapter 25

Critical Thinking

Religious and Spiritual Development

In the "certainty" of historical events that defined my young life, I recall tidbits of life moments that occurred at home, at school, or out and about which germinated religious knowledge and spirituality.

In the Western world, when we speak about religion, the conversation supports language and faith written in the Scriptures. The Bible, "explains" dogma to follow in each Christian religion, based on Jesus Christ and Abraham as savior, and God as deity.

Cuba is traditionally a Catholic country. The Roman Catholic religion was brought to Cuba by Spanish colonialists at the beginning of the 16th century and was the most prevalent professed faith until 1959, when Fidel Castro's Revolution took power.

Upon his triumphant entry into Havana, Castro initially faked his personal religious preference and belief by wearing allegoric Christian jewelry---crucifixes, the rosary, and the cross with or without Jesus around his neck. Although he was baptized and raised a Roman Catholic, he was not a practicing Catholic. Pope John XXIII excommunicated Castro in 1962 after he suppressed Catholic institutions in Cuba.

Sociopolitical history was shaped by popular norms and beliefs that molded the national ethos. Most prominent among them was Santería, a Spanish word that means "the way of saints." Its sacred language is the Lucumí language, a variety of Yoruba.

The Yoruba people carried with them various religious customs: trance and divination to communicate with their ancestors; deities; animal sacrifice; and sacred drumming and dance.

Most Cubans never practiced these rituals, only High Priests called *santeros* did. A considerable percentage of people practiced some sort of Santería, believing in the power of saints, encouraging their support by venerating their image, pleading to them when they sensed a need for help from above.

Most of my Catholic education came at La Salle school in El Vedado, a suburb of Havana. I attended mass, in Latin, twice per week, and more often than that during Catholic holydays like Christmas, Good Friday, Easter Sunday, All Saint's Day, and *Misa de Gallo*--- "Rooster's Mass", also Misa de los Pastores--- "Shepherds' Mass" celebrated on Christmas Eve at midnight.

In Catholicism, each day of the year is assigned to one or more saints, and each person is assigned a patron saint according to their name. This practice played a major role in ancient Judaism. There is a similar Islamic belief in the mu'aqqibat. According to many Muslims, each person has two guardian angels, one in front of and behind while the two recorders are located to the right and left. Meanwhile, a significant Chinese immigration introduced theories and practices of Confucianism.

Mother was a typical Cuban woman, imbued with mixed religious traditions. Yet, she was a devout Catholic, a religion that worships many saints but venerates one deity. Today, in Cuba, Santeros outnumber Catholics eight to one.

Superboy--- Mom, did you practice Santería? I saw your figures of the Virgin Mary, Jesus, the apostles and saints, and the Pope on the table with the candles lit up whenever a celestial request was needed; isn't that Santería?

Mom's Ghost--- Orlando, are you crazy? How could you say such *disparate* (folly)?

This ambivalence influenced the substance of things I believed and hoped for, the evidence of things not seen was shaken---i.e., my faith in God was shaken. As I moved along, I slowly became a doubter of anything unphysical. No particular interest to pursue *"en el más allá"* (in the beyond), especially as a young adult while moving through medical school and learning embryology, anatomy, physiology, pharmacology, chemistry, and physics; my convictions no longer included the certainty of God's existence.

Based on spiritual apprehension rather than proof, Catholic dogma teachings claimed knowledge of the unknowable, contradictory and irrational. "It is what it is," Mom would exclaim. "Faith in God is not a type of knowledge; it is belief without reason." Adding, "My trust and confidence in the existence of the Lord, and the certainty of his presence among us, assures me of His protection."

While I was still in Cuba, Christian faith solidified my strong belief in God and the doctrines of the Catholic Church as taught both at La Salle School and at home. Mother was convinced of an "undeniable truth," a doctrine not later transferred to my laic American public-school education. MBSHS was primarily Jewish and offered no course in Catholic religion.

There is a time and a place for everything real or imagined. As I grew mentally, ideas of religion negatively solidified in disdain for falsity and what I perceived as a devious preconceived agenda controlled by the Catholic Church to influence a population.

I saw many "believers" attend Sunday mass in Madrid, some hiding their bodies with long gray or black dresses and stockings, the faces covered by a *mantilla* (lace veil) with or without gloved hands holding a rosary. Others, flashing jewels, dressed in haute fashion couture parading wealth and power. Were they acting to impress, obeying century-old mores and customs, or was this a sincere reflection of deeply held beliefs? It felt as if they were showing off. I tagged them as liars. Tell me, Jesus, was I right to doubt?

God--- *Orlando. Ay, Orlando. Cuando eras feto, venías con el alma blanca. Siempre supe que tu serías uno de mis más fervientes seguidores.* (Orlando, Oh Orlando. When you were a fetus, it was obvious your soul was white. I always knew you would be one of my most fervent followers.) Becoming Superboy has been tough, hasn't it?

Orlando--- How did you know?

God--- I know everything. I know you have a female side, erotic and sensitive, and a brutal and violent male mirror. I also know you are a liar, a cheat, and (your words) a coward. Rest assured, I will forgive your sins if you repent through confession and ask for forgiveness using prayer and holy acts.

Orlando--- Have you forgiven me for smoking and masturbating at age twelve?

God--- Yes, long ago.

Orlando--- I want to get to know you. Religion teachers at La Salle del Vedado called this "Revelation."

God--- I offer myself to everyone through my son, Jesus Christ, and the *"Espíritu Santo"* (Sancti Spiritus), *rúaj* (in Hebrew), and *pnéuma* (in Greek), the "way" through which I communicate with the world.

Orlando--- I sense I will only know you if I open my heart to you.

God--- I don't believe you are strong enough to do that alone, let me help you.

Orlando--- I am not convinced of anything, but I sense a need to have you in my life. My question to you is, how come---being the omnipotent force for good most religions hold you to be---you allowed this to happen?

God--- I suppose by "this" you are referring to your family's misfortune from losing their country. I am neither a force for good nor evil, right, or wrong, love or hate, rationality or stupidity. I am both the Creator and the Destroyer. If you believe in me, your soul will be saved.

Orlando--- Every religion calls you by a different name. Is that true?

God--- A belief is true if, and only if, it is part of a coherent system of beliefs.

Mom's Ghost--- Son, faith is a strong conviction that cannot be questioned or proven right or wrong by physical basis and deductions, that reigns in the minds and spirit of the faithful.

Orlando--- God, I believe in You, but I also believe in my parents. My mother always said I had a "white" soul. She said:

"*Hijo mío, tú tienes un alma blanca.*" But what does that mean? Do black people have a white soul too?

God--- Having a white soul means your soul is clean and pure, exempt from malignancies in thought or intent. Black people, as well as other white people, and all human races also have that. At least, some of them do.

Orlando--- Either way, when I was growing up in Miramar I was known as a "smart ass" *(mojón de mierda, un listo de los cojones.).* I enjoyed sharing my "grandiose" opinion with anyone who had the patience to listen. Was I sinning?

God--- You were extremely perceptive. You saw yourself as a visionary, felt others didn't see with clarity what you "saw" was to come. You were merely Superboy, an amazing kid with previously unknown superpower, Superman in the making, not quite God.

Orlando--- You are a man, aren't you? Most believe and trust in their loyalty to you certain their faith to be male centered.

God--- Their belief in something for which there is no proof, clings to the faith professed in the traditional doctrines of a religion. For example, Islam. "Righteous is he who believes in Allah and the Last Day and the Angels and the Scriptures and the Prophets." — *Qur'an 2:177*

Mom's Ghost--- *Esto expone la varianza y el aislamiento que caracterizan a las religiones del mundo.* (This exposes the variance and isolation characterizing world religions.)

God--- *No hay dos religiones en armonía o de acuerdo entre sí.* (No two religions are in harmony or agreement with each other)---although many similarities exist among them.

Mom's Ghost--- *Un conflicto amargo, a veces violento se produjo con frecuencia en la contención por la superioridad espiritual.* (A bitter, sometimes violent conflict frequently ensued in contention for spiritual superiority.)

God--- Both meaning, and intent remain blurred, increasing arguments (in favor of non-believers) that support my nonexistence. But I am still and will forever be here.

Orlando--- Many of those who subscribe to or advocate atheism believed in You and stopped after a long and arduous process of discovery, examination, questioning, and thought in the faith they had professed to over many years, now feeling it is not true.

God--- Of course! Atheists argue that removing the notion of an afterlife, helps us grasp the reality and beauty of this life.

Mom's Ghost--- *Pero, la creencia en Ti no niega la belleza del planeta ni sus habitantes.* (But belief in You does not deny the beauty of the planet nor its inhabitants.)

Orlando--- My biggest issue with faith is the question: Am I going to see Dad and Mom when I pass?

Mom's Ghost--- *Por supuesto que nos veremos, y te daré muchos besitos.* (Of course, we will see each other again, and I will give you many kisses.)

God--- In Luke 24:13-35 I speak of Resurrection through my son and his disciples.

Mom's Ghost--- According to the most ancient texts such as the Bible, Torah, Talmud, and the Sumerian Tablets, You created a man [genesis] directly by blowing dust from the ground up into his nostrils, converting a lifeless form into a living being. This is consistent with Sacred Scripture, as taught by Saint Thomas Aquinas. We owe You everything.

Superboy--- I wonder if that was God's greatest contribution to humanity.

Mom's Ghost--- Not really. His greatest contribution was when He created a woman.

Orlando--- Mom, who was Saint Thomas Aquinas?

Mom's Ghost--- He was an Italian Dominican friar, Catholic priest, and Doctor of the Church.

God--- He is an immensely influential philosopher theologian, and jurist in the tradition of scholasticism.

Orlando--- Do you expect me to know what that word means?

Mom's Ghost--- It is a method of *critical thought*.

Orlando--- Was he critical of everybody the way you were with Humberto?

Mom's Ghost--- Your brother was okay. You did have to listen to him and do what he said.

Orlando--- Are you kidding me?

Humberto's Ghost--- Shut up, Orlando; just listen without interruption. Let Mom speak.

Mom's Ghost--- What else do you want to know, Superboy? I am quite busy.

Orlando--- So, what is critical thought?

Mom's Ghost--- Learning to be proper.

Orlando--- What does that mean?

Mom's Ghost--- Behaving with learned holy scriptures, which always leads to strengthening self-image propriety and performance.

Orlando--- How the hell do you do that?

God--- If you pray and read the Bible, your life will have more meaning.

Mom reminded us every time we sat down to dinner not to serve more food on our plate than that which we were planning to consume. Today, my sister Ana Maria's favored prayer to fight gluttony and greed and promote charity and kindness is offered at every family meal.

Ana María's Prayer --- "Señor, Gracias por los Alimentos que vamos a tomar. Dale Pan a los que tengan Hambre, Y Hambre de Ti a los que tengan pan" (Lord, thank you for the food we are going to consume. Give Bread to those who are Hungry, and Hunger for You to those who have Bread.)

Orlando— Isn't religion the greatest reason for so many wars where millions of people were displaced from their homes to die in a foreign land?

God--- You are so inquisitive! Yes, religion causes war, a matter of historical fact. Since time immemorial, men have fought each other in wars caused by religion.

Orlando--- That sounds like the Middle East war between Jews and Arabs. What if all world religions positioned themselves voluntarily as "parallel-wave" clouds, each cloud representing a religion? They all travel in the same direction with a common purpose, but never touch, maybe out of respect for the other. God, if You have an opinion about which doctrine is right, why don't You say so? Why can't human beings get along?

God--- Ask Superboy.

Chapter 26
"Chaval" Español

We had arrived in Spain.

Dad--- *No te preocupes, Chonita, todo saldrá bien.* (Don't worry, Chonita, all will be alright.)

Mom--- *Cómo puedes estar tan seguro?* (How can you be so sure?)

Our parents' decision in 1963 to move from the US to Spain was complicated and triggered by several events affecting our safety and growth as a family. Humberto had finished his freshman year at the University of Miami, and I had graduated from Miami Beach Senior High School two months before I turned seventeen. Two years earlier, Mother's youngest brother, Uncle Chirrino was killed at the Bay of Pigs. Mom was convinced that Humberto and I would join the revolutionary effort to overthrow Castro's Revolution.

The Cuban community in exile in Miami worked hard to get our patriots back home from Cuban jails. There were one hundred and seventy-six killed by Cuban armed forces. One hundred and eighteen were from the Brigade 2506, including Chirrino. Castro's National Militia suffered two thousand killed and wounded.

Four American citizens lost their lives in the conflict, organized, and supported by the Brigade 2506, the CIA, the US

Air Force, and the US Navy. As the invaders lost the strategic initiative, the international community found out about the invasion, and US President John F. Kennedy decided to withhold further air support triggering the failure of the mission. This disaster impacted Mom's decision to leave the country.

Mom's Ghost--- The whole family pleaded with Chirri to stay home and raise a family. He was young, adventurous, and very courageous, intent on achieving freedom for Cuba. A true patriot, my baby brother went to his death with honor. It broke our hearts.

There were other significant reasons, like the increasingly liberal tendencies in our society. Mom was a conservative, unaccustomed to fashions and behaviors, a severe critic of the uncontrolled lifestyle I was favoring. Her difficulty assimilating these major changes in her environment made her increasingly insecure. The stress was heightened by the robbery of Dad's business in Wynwood.

At that time, Dad was unable to get around unassisted, requiring a cane to walk. He had been in an "accident" a year earlier as he exited his parked car in front of his business, Jomares Market on Northwest Twenty-fourth Street and North Miami Avenue in Wynwood, Florida. Mother's version was that an elderly man did not see him come out of the car. Our suspicion was that he was a victim of a professional "job." Not long before the accident, Dad was at the checkout counter when three men entered Jomares Market and took all the cash and his watch while pointing a rifle at him.

As they left, Dad took his gun and ran after them, shooting one of them in the butt. Being a marksman, he could have easily killed them, but he did not shoot to kill. We believe the perpetrators, contracted by the men who had robbed his store a month earlier, intentionally ran over him. The family was ready to move to a safer environment. Dad's sister, Carmen {Chely, Tía Tá} already lived in Madrid and enjoyed an exceedingly high standard of living. Mauro, her husband, owned several five and six-star Michelin restaurants, including Las Lanzas, the best restaurant in Madrid, Breda, and a very select men's bar, Zosca

Before departing Miami Beach, Mother gave us a preview of the world to come when arriving in Madrid. She knew we were all leaving important things and people behind. I was "temporarily" traveling out of the country, but "it wouldn't be long" before I saw Madeline again.

Mom--- *Chely nos está esperando. Ella me asegura que la vida en Madrid es muy tranquila y sosegada, que la seguridad ciudadana y nacional está garantizada, y los valores cívicos defendidos por un gobierno eficiente.* (Your aunt is waiting for us. She assures me that life in Madrid is peaceful and calm, that both, public safety, and national security are guaranteed, and civil values are defended by an efficient government.)

Dad--- *Yo sé que los niños lograrán salir adelante, pero es un mundo nuevo para ellos, igual que lo fué cuando llegamos a Miami en el 59.* (I know the boys will be fine, but it will be a new world for them, just as it was when we arrived in Miami in 59.)

Humberto and I traveled ahead of the family to Chely's home. The advantages of living in Europe, better education; broader, more diverse culture; amazing history in the arts, architecture, and literature; and a more tolerant and safer lifestyle became a magnet difficult to reject. We were excited to discover what awaited us.

Our arrival at Barajas Airport in Madrid was a shock.

Two American teenagers [us] were instructed to look for a gray Mercedes-Benz driven by their chauffeur, Félix, who would be wearing a gray uniform. He spotted us first. His obsequiousness to serve our needs approached servilism. It was a venal disrespect, initially gratifying as we both perceived an offer to help with our luggage.

We were soon to be enlightened by a customary behavior typical of Spanish social status strata at the time. As high school students in Miami Beach, we learned the rich American has no grandeur; the poor man no servility; human relations in daily life are on a footing of equality.

Félix--- *Hola, chicos! Venid, aquí estoy!* (Hello, children! Come, I am here!)

He was yelling and beckoning us to him. We moved gingerly toward the car, expecting to enjoy the benefits of a ride in a chauffeured Mercedes.

Humberto--- *Usted es Félix?* (You are Félix?)
Félix--- *Sí, sí, vengan, vengan.* (Yes, yes, come, come.)

Félix opened the right rear car door, then bent at the waist, downward and forward. I assumed this was a gesture used to cordially greet a visitor or recent arrival. He took all our bags, placing them in the trunk. Félix appeared excited and joyfully welcoming, which transferred a loving message, to greet us hospitably with courtesy and cordiality, a welcomed respite from a long flight.

As we proceeded along the highway from Barajas Airport and down the dusty streets of Madrid filled with speeding small cars, mostly taxis, the only significant difference I noticed was his accent, different in many ways from our Cuban spoken Spanish. All three of us spoke Castilian, as opposed to Basque, Catalonian, or other Spanish languages, but the distinction presented more dissimilarity in pronunciation than form.

Spaniards pronounce the letter "C" similar to the way Cubans pronounce the letter "Z" (the tongue protruding through the front teeth), and they pronounce the letter "J" gargled from the throat, as opposed to softly "blown" as exhaled. The delivery of every word, phrase, or sentence was considerably more forceful. This discrepancy in attitude and communication dimmed the feeling that the man was subservient to his boss and his relatives or friends. As the chauffer spoke, Humberto looked at me, and I smiled, lifting my shoulders in a sign of wonder.

Félix--- *Ya hemos llegado, chicos* (We have arrived, kids.)

Our aunt and uncle lived with their children, Maurito and Lourdes (Lula), and Mauro's parents, Blanca and Jesús, in a very high-end neighborhood in Madrid. Their penthouse condo was huge, in a privileged area behind the Prado Museum, overlooking the Retiro Park---equal to Central Park in New York City. Las Lanzas was located on the first floor and basement of the building, occupying twenty thousand square feet.

On arrival to my uncle and aunt's condo building, the chauffeur again bowed in reverence and courtesy, grabbed our luggage, and ran to open all doors from the car through the building entrance to the lobby and finally to the elevator doors, each time repeating the welcoming procedure in that sequential order. We were floored by a salute that appeared a gesture or other action used to reference the arrival of dignitaries in a visit to a monarchical head of state. We were confused. He was being nice and helpful, but...

Was it a display of respect or gratitude? Never in my wildest dreams could I expect the words that followed: *Bienvenidos a España, "señoritos."* For those speaking a different language, señoritos translates into "Master" or "Rich Young Man." To us, it sounded like he was calling us small misters or tiny men, but what bothered me was his repeated forward inclination as he bent at the hip in obvious intent to show us as superior to him. I wondered if his next accolade could be: "Would his lordship allow me to help him? I presume he doesn't want to get dirty?" He had bowed thrice. Humberto and I looked at each other again, confused and holding back a giggle.

Orlando--- Mom, why did we move to Madrid?
Mom's Ghost--- At the time, your father and I were convinced Madrid, supported by his sister Chely, who had moved there in 1958, would bring stability and the opportunity to start a new business. We would also be closer to you and your brother and help with the start of your medical careers.

We went up to the penthouse to meet the family. Waiting was the maid, who opened the door and welcomed us, less servile than Félix, but still overly respectful, like a butler.

Maid--- *Su tía está esperando en el salón; ella está impaciente por verlos.* (Your aunt is waiting in the living room; she can't wait to see you.)

The maid took our bags, and we moved toward Tía Tá, my favored and most beloved aunt. With that great smile, shining with love and affection, she stood with open arms to receive our hugs and kisses.

Orlando--- *Hola, Tía! Como estás? Te ves bien.* (Hello, Aunt! How are you? You look good.)
Chely--- *Maurito y Lula ya salieron para el colegio.* (Maurito and Lula have already left for school.)
Humberto--- *Y Mauro?* (And Mauro?)
Chely— *Está en el baño.* (He is in the bathroom).
Orlando--- *Ay, Tía, que lindo está tu apartamento! Qué ganas tenía de verte.* (Oh, Auntie, what a beautiful apartment! I was so looking forward to seeing you.)

Chely was such a kind person. She overflowed with love and affection; carried the biggest heart in the family. I loved her as much as I did Mom, or [sometimes] more—but I did not dare to tell either. Mother was keenly jealous of her. But Tía Tá had serious problems at home. Mauro was not an easy husband, but he was a good father, an excellent provider, and felt the deepest interpersonal affection for Chely, his children, and his parents.

It took only one week for Mauro to "help" us find somewhere else to live. He was unhappy with two "American" teens breaking his daily routine. Humberto and I had immediately begun playing the nightlife offered in the Spanish capital. Jazz clubs closed at 4 a.m., and that is when we returned to Chely's condo.

Mauro had excellent connections, having no trouble finding his two [wild] teenagers [us] luxury living quarters to hang our clothes.

It was La Casa do Brasil (The House of Brazil), the best fraternity house in Madrid. It was plush, brand new, and wild; we adapted immediately. We studied and played as much as we could, and we met wonderful young people from Brazil and other South American countries, as well as many Europeans who studied in Madrid. It was the Spanish version of a European-sophisticated "Animal House."

The dorm buildings were divided, one occupied by girls, the other by boys, but that didn't prevent mingling. I kept lying to Brazilian women about my shyness and lack of experience with girls. They all wanted to protect my fragility. For a couple of months, we "survived" in the Brazilian paradise, as male and female students traveled undercover of dimmed night lights inside the dorms.

My parents arrived in Madrid two months later following a transatlantic voyage, Fort Lauderdale, Florida to Vigo, Spain, bringing my grandmother Esperanza and my sister Ana Maria with them. They rented an apartment near the University of Madrid, and we moved in, enjoying once again the comfort and safety of our home. Shortly, we began to socialize while learning our way around the Spanish capital.

Our studies would begin at the University of Madrid. Humberto preferred medicine, whereas I, having taken four years of mechanical drawing in high school, leaned toward architecture and the arts. Hence, he enrolled in the School of

Medicine and I in the School of Architecture with a minor in aeronautical engineering. I also dreamed of being a pilot, like Chirrino. Not much later, I would transfer to the School of Medicine.

Humberto's Ghost--- I envied you and your life-course. I'm the one who should have become a Doctor in Medicine in my younger years. It took me a lifetime.

Orlando--- You chose to pursue business interests when I chose to go back to medical school.

Mom's Ghost--- Humberto, you shouldn't speak like that to your brother. Be kind and just and accept the decision you made.

Humberto's Ghost--- I spent a lifetime being friendly, generous, and considerate. He effortlessly made it, thanks to me.

God--- Anger makes you weaker. Jealousy destroys the soul.

Orlando--- Effortlessly? You, better than anyone, should know how difficult it is to graduate from medical school. Like you said, "it literally took you a lifetime."

Things were tough for both of us, but we were young and full of energy and ambition. I admired his amazing successes at Procter & Gamble, while at the same time leading Maquelsa S.A., our vending machine business while frequently traveling to and from Zaragoza for medical school testing. We turned a small operation into a medium-sized family business, thanks to Humberto's outstanding commitment to excellence. Nothing came easy.

Humberto's Ghost--- I never left your side. I always had your back. You knew I was there for you. No matter where we went, we were stronger together.

Orlando--- I can't deny your concern for my safety and welfare. I felt we could conquer the world together, and we did just that through our teen years, but then everything broke down.

Humberto's Ghost--- Something happened that I cannot understand, but I know things got worse between us.

He and Cristina Olivares (La Gallega) met in Madrid shortly, a couple of months after our arrival to Spain in late 1963. I was already looking to transfer to medicine, University of Zaragoza. She was a high school senior; we were premed students cohabiting in the building where Mom and Dad rented an apartment in a preppy area of town, near La Ciudad Universitaria (University City). She was gorgeous, a cheeky freckled face, smooth shiny white skin, a Mona Lisa-suggestive smile with eyes rising innocently on a search for gay lust. Exceptionally long, straight light brunette hair hung softly back well beyond and between her shoulders. Her parents, dad an engineer, mom a traditional "Spanish" housewife, did not like Humberto.

Orlando--- Do you think I felt jealous about your sudden focus-switch from me to La Gallega when you fell in love with her? Well, I did. I was seventeen and you eighteen when you laid your eyes on her.

It was the first time Humberto turned his primary focus away from me onto another person. My brother's feelings were hurt when Cristina left him two years later. The bitter indignation at having been rejected, treated unfairly, created resentment, a mixture of disappointment, disgust, anger, and fear triggering secondary emotions that altered his mood. I wished he would have listened to his younger brother trying to soothe his spirit as he experienced prejudice, when I suggested to him: "Don't take the engineer's dismissal and Cristina's rebuff seriously."

However, "don't take it personal" comments, even well-intentioned, may become subliminal messages implying "it's not that big a loss," an insult that may lead to even greater injury to self-image, especially when a fracturing event occurs. By providing an escape route for saving face, the face he saved may have just gotten a little uglier.

By accepting defeat, a weakened image of who we were emerged. I knew we had all been rejected, not just Humberto. As we traveled from Cuba to the United States and now to Spain, we each encountered premeditated judgments from others who saw only our surface: Cuban exiles.

We were not the first immigrants to move to that building but had to prove our commitment to values similar to those held by Cristina's family. There was a measurable image to be developed, a look-alike of those locals studying our every move. We had been there before, in Culver, GES, and Beach High.

Which virtues were more meaningful to those neighbors observing our behavior as we came home from school or work? Meeting *el portero* (the doorman) at the lobby or a nearby resident in the elevator introduced opportunities to encourage friendship and discourage enmity. However, "it takes two to tango," and time to complete the dance. We did not get used to each other overnight. Superboy was beginning his *Super "Niño"* adolescent stage in a new country, with weird norms.

John Fitzgerald Kennedy had been shot. The world was still reeling from it, "the Event of the Decade," shared with man's moon landing six years later. Vietnam was brewing.

The new Spanish experience required a transformation, to speak with *acento madrileño* (a Spanish accent typical of Madrid) and dress formally in coat and tie, nothing like the madras bermuda shorts and sneakers outfit I sported previously while living in Miami Beach. The music and the dancing were a bigger challenge, whereas the food and drinking, mostly wine, beer, and vermouth at the *tascas* (neighborhood bars displaying huge appetizers called *tapas),* was a definite improvement from Royal Castle, Burger King, and Beach High cafeteria food. A new language sprouted as we continued to speak "Spanish" using new words. *Una "caña" de cerveza* meant a glass of draft beer; *un "chato" de vino*, a glass of wine, *"tinto"* (red), *"blanco"* (white) or *"clarete"* (merlot). No longer, *Spanglish.*

From the day we left Cuba, several major losses were tallied, as we struggled to find footing in the Old World. Mom and Dad losing almost everything they worked so hard to build, the bitterness of Chirrino's loss at the Bay of Pigs, and Dad's challenges to get around assisted by a cane. His work ethic was amazing, almost as committed as the friendship and kindness offered anyone in need of help. His last rodeo was four years away.

Chapter 27
I Meet Mary Carmen

Orlando / Mary Carmen

"You know you're in love when you can't fall asleep because reality is finally better than your dreams."

---Dr. Seuss

In my attempt to achieve a fabulous superfamily filled with many Superboys and Supergirls of our making, my own Superwoman---Mary Carmen---showed up. She came into this world May 6, 1949, approximately two years and nine months after my birth.

Coincidentally, her sister, Norma, was born August 24, 1946, my birthday, the same day and in the same hospital in Havana where my mother delivered me. You heard right! Virginia---my future mother-in-law---delivered Mary Carmen's sister, Norma, the day I was born! The two mothers were friends in the Havana of the 1940s, years before their pregnancy.

Norma and I celebrated each other's birthdays together while her sister was in a crib or toddling around. Mary Carmen was fourteen when we met as teenagers in Madrid, where she lived with her family and I studied medicine. Our youth and sensitivities embraced a lifelong relationship that still lives strong after six decades.

How we met is a typical story of old fairy tales, where a family seeks a partner for the children and the search intensifies as the kids get closer to marrying age. That is how Maria's mother, Virginia, paid a visit to my mother, Chona, at our Madrid apartment to welcome her to Spain.

There was a multitude of parallelisms in our families' histories and relationships. During Virginia's visit, after all the "proper" small talk about the vicissitudes that defined each other's life since leaving Cuba where they had been good friends, my mother-in-law-to-be asked my mother the question she had come to ask:

Virginia--- *Qué hacen tus hijos?* (What are your boys up to?)
Mom--- *Qué quieres decir?* (What do you mean?)
Virginia--- *Qué es lo que hacen con su tiempo libre cuando no están estudiando medicina?* (What are they doing with their free time when they are not studying medicine?)
Mom--- *Nada bueno.* (They are up to no good.)

Mom was always somewhat proud of her boys' perilous activities, impetuous behaviors, and stormy young lives.

That should have been the end of it, but the conversation continued with Virginia's interest, secretly shared by my mother, in bringing their progeny together. After all, who better than us, their children, to meet and become friends, hopefully developing a relationship that---who knows?---might end up in matrimony. They were acting as marriage brokers, matchmakers to our union.

The request came for my brother and me to pay a visit to the Gómez home to meet the girls, Maria del Carmen, and Norma. Humberto chickened out that day. He and Cristina had been together for five months. I was still in a long-distance relationship with Madeline. Choosing to stay home, Humberto did not go to Virginia's home. I made the opposite decision.

No two situations are equal, though they may be similar according to the context in which they exist. Meeting the love of my life was a planned event, but it hinged on both of our families inhabiting the same city at the same time.

As I went up to the third floor in the old elevator, a feeling of nervous anticipation engulfed me, a sensation of excitement waiting eagerly for something I knew was about to happen: *the luckiest day in my life.*

I exited the lift; I looked left and then right, trying to find Apartment C. I walked slowly and knocked on the door. I rang the bell and there she was, a stunningly beautiful angel, a young woman kindly smiling in a welcoming gesture.

She said,

Mary Carmen--- *Hola, tú eres Orlando?* (Hello, are you Orlando?)

I thought, no! I am Superboy!

Never could I have dreamed I was meeting "the one" who would become my loving, adoring, life partner. I fell in love immediately, in April 1964, with my new guardian angel. She would fill my life with all things good. Mary Carmen asked me to be her date at her Fifteenth Birthday party, May 5, 1964; an honor for any young woman seeking introduction into society.

We stayed together throughout our youth in Madrid, then in Puerto Rico, and finally in the US. On July 12 2019, we celebrated our 50th Wedding Anniversary.

I began acting more grownup; after all, I was in college now, and Mary Carmen was my fiancée. La Facultad de Medicina de Madrid, located in Madrid's University City, was a huge stone and redbrick building with large gray concrete slabs stepping up to reach the massive wood and steel door behind the tallest columns I had ever seen. It made me feel like a little person, walking between them to enter the dark, humid, cold (classes began in the late fall) lobby where imposing paintings of world-renowned "maestros" hung proudly on the walls.

Since girls tend to enter puberty before boys, the Spanish girls I met appeared more likely to experience the wave of crushes first, more drawn to boys than boys were to them, taking romantic feelings more seriously than boys, who often chose to treat them lightly. The move to a more controlled social environment was not far off. It all happened spontaneously, at Mary Carmen's friend's house party, a somewhat formal teen dance event chaperoned by adults.

A romantic crush is a potent mix of idealization and infatuation: it doesn't require knowing another person well at all. In some cases, a superficial impression can be provocation enough. "I like how he's so quiet and watchful and keeps to himself." That is how Mary Carmen probably perceived me when she spotted me looking out her friend's living room window into the dark of night. I was probably homesick, maybe missing Madeline. "I like how what others think doesn't matter to him," she may have thought, as I ignored everyone at the party.

Although her crush appeared to be about physical attraction, it was actually about a projection of valued attributes onto me. Sound familiar? It was a statement not about me but about what she found attractive. Another attachment transfer, from brother to girlfriend and wife, was in the making.

We began dating, always chaperoned and mostly by her sister Norma. Mary Carmen and family were part of a Cuban-Hispanic group of friends who frequented Gómez's new bar/restaurant in Madrid, El Pollo Blanco (The White Chicken), where I would often go to see her and plan the weekend around group activities. We stayed close, even after Humberto and I transferred to Zaragoza Medical School, 321 kilometers from Madrid. It was a four-hour train ride, but for young lovers, it felt we had moved to the opposite end of the planet. During those difficult times, we remained attached, *uña y carne*, as nail to nailbed.

Our love affair, different from the one I experienced with Madeline, brought stability and peace to both of us. We needed each other. In parallel to my desire to fit in with those American teens at Beach High, I longed for a similar incorporation into Mary Carmen's group of friends in Madrid. In doing so, I did not feel as challenged. To the contrary, they embraced me and facilitated our interaction. They were now the solvent for me to dissolve into. It still required adaptation.

Chapter 28
Dad Dies

Orlando--- *Papá, te estás muriendo* (Dad, you are dying...)

It is all I could think about.

It was winter 1964. We were all happy and content with the life we enjoyed in Madrid. Four quick months had passed for Humberto and me since arriving to the Spanish capital in early September 1963. We were already underway with our freshman year at the school of medicine. By then, we knew enough about the city to move about at will and not get lost, and it was easier to mingle with the locals. Many places we visited began to feel familiar. Tapas bars, cafeterias and restaurants, movie theaters, jazz clubs, museums, department stores, and fraternity houses became frequent stops when not studying.

Madrid had so many things to offer. The Prado Museum, famous around the world for its majestic architecture and awe-inspiring permanent collections of Velazquez, Goya, El Greco, Murillo, Picasso, Dali, and many others. Its river (Rio Manzanares), El Parque del Retiro, and multiple plazas bustling with energy and delightful people. La Puerta del Sol, right in the center of Madrid, an iconic landmark of the city and possibly Spain's busiest square, is where all subway trains enter and leave at the Central 5-story transfer station. It is also from where all road distances North, South, East, and West are measured, in the Iberian peninsula since the time of the Romans.

History appeared to be more relevant in Europe than in the US. The iconic Bronze Bear statue at the center of La Puerta del Sol is surrounded by the rest of the city which spreads out rippling, like a rock hitting the water, transferring its energy to the surroundings. For the next three years, Dad worked tirelessly. In Madrid, he opened several businesses in that short time span. In continued service to his countrymen, other Cuban exiles arriving in dire circumstances, he spent days and weeks at the US Embassy helping them obtain visas to travel to their destination, the United States.

Orlando--- *Mamá, me voy a la Embajada con Papá* (Mom, I am going to the Embassy with Dad.)
Mom--- *Tengan cuidado. No se demoren* (Be careful. Don't delay.)
Orlando--- *Papá, nos vamos en tranvía?* (Dad, are we leaving by tram?)

Following the metro or subway, rail trams were the second most popular mode of transportation in Madrid. I adored trains, especially the sounds of steel-on-steel squeaking on the cobblestone streets of the capital. The breeze through the open glass windows loudly screamed every gust as the old wood frames bounced on slightly bent pieces of steel, screeching at every stop. Frequent stops made the ride ever more interesting, giving everyone time to look at those entering and exiting the wagon.

Upon arrival at the Embassy, Dad got off first, holding the door handle with one hand and his walking cane with the other. Armed with a smile, he looked back to me and exclaimed,

Dad--- *Orlando, ya llegamos. Estamos un poco tarde* (Orlando, we are here. We're a bit late.)

Orlando--- *Tarde?*

Dad--- *El Señor García*—no relation to us---*nos está esperando* (Mr. García is waiting for us.)

General Consul at the US Embassy in Madrid, García was in charge of all legal human traffic between Spain and the US.

Orlando--- Dad, is he in charge of the Embassy?

Dad--- No. The American ambassador is in charge. El Señor García is responsible for the issue of visas to enter the United States.

As we walked into the huge lobby, Dad characteristically looked to his right, then to his left. He usually found someone he knew, but more frequently someone who knew Dad would spot him and come forward to speak to him. Dad enjoyed helping others and knew this short delay would give a person in need the opportunity to approach him. Once together, the person seeking help, sensing Dad's need for brevity, typically spoke much of what he needed to say in seconds, as an "elevator pitch."

Cuban Exile --- *Sr. Garcia, me llamo "fulano de tal"* (so-and-so) *y necesito su ayuda en ésto o aquéllo.* (and I need your help in this or that...)

A look, then a breath, and on he went just as quickly,

Cuban Exile --- *Somos ocho, cuatro adultos, tres niños y un bebé.* (We are eight, four adults, three children and a baby.)

Dad asked him how long he and his family had been waiting there, as he took the man's papers and pictures and all items relevant to immigration to show them to Señor García.

Señor Garcia--- *Hola Humberto. Ya veo que tienes algo para mí. Sé que esa familia lleva aquí cuatro o cinco días. Como vés, estamos muy ocupados.* (Hello Humberto. I see you have something for me. I know that family has been here four or five days. As you can see, we are terribly busy.)

Dad--- *Llevan tres días sin comer más que un bocadillo para cada uno de los adultos al mediodía. Los niños y el bebé bebieron un poco de leche esta mañana, pero sólo una manzana ayer. Tenemos que hacer algo hoy a más tardar, antes de que se enfermen.* (They have not eaten for three days, except for a sandwich today at noon. The children and the baby had some milk and an apple yesterday. We must do something before they become ill.)

Señor Garcia---*Hoy mismo me pongo a trabajar en ello.* (I will begin working on it today.)

On our way out...

Dad--- *Orlando, esta noche vámos al aeropuerto a llevar ropa y abrigos a los exilados que llegan por avión a Barajas.* (Orlando, tonight we will go to Barajas—Madrid' airport--to help Cuban exiles who need clothes.)

My father continued his business pursuits, while my brother and I kept busy with school and other endeavors. As we began to look for leisure activities to fill our time away from classes and studying, sports reentered the top priority on our to-do list.

* * * * *

Baseball began as a sport relatively early in Spain, thanks to the descendants of immigrants from Cuba. They brought it along with them when Cuba ceased to be a Spanish colony. The heyday of baseball in Spain was in the 1950s (post Korean War) and 1960s. Owing to mass interest in *futbol* (soccer) many baseball clubs didn't survive into the 1970s. Multiple TV channels were focused mainly on broadcasting the professional First Division Spanish National Soccer League, "La Liga," games featuring their national sport. It was unreasonable to expect the public's massive shift in attention to embrace a relatively new sport. One of the few survivors from the early *béisbol* experience was the CB Viladecans; their field was officially used during the 1992 Summer Olympics in Barcelona.

At the Ciudad Universitaria, the only sport offered was rugby, played at the University stadium located behind Casa do Brasil. Our team's [Medicine] roster included only participants drawn from the student body. Having played high school football, a sport similar to rugby with comparable rules and an oblong-shaped leather ball, Humberto and I excelled immediately. But baseball was where our hearts were.

We began to ask questions to family and students, at bars and in taxi cabs, anywhere we went. No one had ever heard of an official baseball league in town. There was no Google to ask the question and get an answer.

Orlando--- We knew that sooner or later we would be playing baseball.

243

Humberto's Ghost--- There was no doubt; whether the sport existed in Spain or not was irrelevant. We knew Dad would help us out.

One day, while shopping at the largest department store in Madrid, El Corte Inglés, we met one of the employees in the sports department who said they carried baseball items. Voilá! There was baseball in Spain! Humberto and I began calling on local baseball fans.

All US military bases play baseball amongst themselves and participate in a competitive league of their own. And there was one in Madrid. The chief military commander stationed at Torrejón Air Base outside Madrid reviewed the plan we presented to develop a baseball league. Appearing impressed with two teenagers in love with "America's pastime," he offered and delivered on his promise to help.

We then paid a visit to Galerías Preciados, at the time the largest department store in the country. Its owner, José "Pepín" Fernández (Galerías Preciados) and Ramón Areces (El Corte Inglés) had been baseball fans in Cuba. They knew Dad well. We arranged a visit. They were both impressed enough with our youth, vitality, and love for the sport to commit their unconditional support to our plan. Supplies and equipment, bats and balls, gloves, and uniforms, including spikes, all free with no request for payback. We held practice sessions at Ciudad Universitaria and soon thereafter at the new Baseball Stadium, built with their money, for the new King's Cup Baseball League.

Our efforts sprung a rebirth of a sport that had been unattended by the Spanish Baseball National Federation.

Humberto made several trips to the Dominican Republic to recruit players. National interest spread and immediate success followed.

Humberto's Ghost --- *El Campeonato de España, Copa del Generalísimo, se llevó a cabo entre los meses de Julio y Octubre 1963, tres meses antes de nuestra llegada a España, y se acordó que la primera eliminatoria fuera de carácter regional. Finalmente, sólo se jugó en Cataluña.* (The Spanish Championship, Copa del Generalísimo [Francisco Franco], was held between July and October 1963, three months before our arrival to Spain, and it was agreed that the first qualifier would be regional. Finally, it was only played in Catalonia.)

La Elipa, a suburb of Madrid, was home to the stadium which had been built exclusively for Spanish baseball. Its construction followed specifications toward that purpose. The stands were made of concrete cement, with seating for five hundred spectators, under roof. The field had the quality grass lawn and finest infield packed-in sand, manicured to perfection, and professionally maintained impeccably for weekly games. Metal halides, the most used field light source for Major League Baseball stadiums in the US and Canada were installed, allowing for night games.

Opening Days were June 29 and 30, 1964. The new baseball field, first of its kind in Spain, scheduled four major teams to compete in a doubleheader on Opening Day: The Castilla and Cataluña All-Stars, and two other teams were representing the Torrejón de Ardoz Air Force Base (Ridder Team), and a fourth representing the Zaragoza Air Force Base (Matador Team).

It rapidly became our Spanish Field of Dreams. So, it happened that baseball was already alive in Spain when we arrived, but we improved the sport with a tremendous effort driven by our love for the game. Humberto played second base for El Corte Inglés during those peak years between 1964 and 1970, his team winning three National Division 1 Championships, and I played third base for Rayo Vallecano, winning the Division 2 National Championship in Vigo, Galicia in 1968.

Humberto's Ghost--- *Sabes qué? Aquí en La Elipa jugarán niños y viejos, y vendrán deportistas de todas partes de España y el Caribe a aprender y a enseñar como jugar pelota. Tenemos que empezar a buscar promotores en los colegios y tiendas por departamento. Verdad, Papá?* (You know what? The young and the old will play ball here, athletes from the whole country and the Caribbean will learn and teach the sport. We need to start looking for promoters among schools and department stores. Right, Dad?)

* * * * *

In November 1966, in the midst of our baseball glory, Dad presented to the emergency room at the local University Hospital with severe acute abdominal pain accompanied by vomiting. He was immediately taken to the operating room where an exploratory laparotomy revealed bowel obstruction. It was probably part of a lung cancer already metastatic, but the surgeons and pathologist failed to pick it up. It was a real shitty Christmas, but we had no idea it would be his last. For several months he had a cough with bloody sputum.

We took Dad to see a cardiothoracic surgeon, Dr Martínez Bourdieú, who was married to Generalísimo Francisco Franco's daughter. He looked at Dad's chest X-ray taken that day and showed Humberto and me the film knowing we were both medical students and could probably read it. At first sight, I failed to see anything significant, but then, I looked a little closer as the doctor asked if dad had had a previous chest film taken within a year.

Dad--- Yes, I had a CXR in November when I had surgery, and maybe two months before, when I had my tonsils taken out. The ENT doctor said the blood came from coughing too hard due to tonsillitis.

After reviewing the films side-by-side, we could see that back in September there was already a shadow, with significant growth in size of this pulmonary mass appearing in the left upper lobe with a high chance of malignancy. Dad was a heavy smoker since his teens, and now that habit was about to kill him.

A call came from Tio Quico's house in Texas, my uncle, Dr. David (Quico) Almeyda was one of Dr Denton Cooley's anesthesiologists. An American heart and cardiothoracic surgeon, famous for performing the first implantation of a total artificial heart, Cooley was founder and surgeon-in-chief of the Texas Heart Institute, and chief of Cardiovascular Surgery at Baylor St. Luke's Medical Center in Houston. He offered to manage Dad's case. Humberto and Mom took Dad to Houston. My brother called me that day to give me details and the bad news from the lung biopsy. He told me Dad was terribly ill and didn't have long to live. "The tumor is a metastatic lung cancer, and it has spread throughout his chest cavity," he sobbingly said.

Humberto's Ghost--- We stopped in Miami, on our way home to Madrid. to say goodbye to our family there.

Three months of cobalt radiation at the Ruber Clinic in Madrid, and Dad was gone. During Dad's last days, Dr Cooley visited him at the clinic. It was an amazing feat Humberto pulled off by following Cooley and the Marquis of Villaverde (Dr. Martínez Bourdieú) along the VIP tour of the capital, through Madrid late at night, to his hotel room, and knocking on the surgeon's door, and then inviting him to "make rounds" on dad. The next morning, Dad's world-renowned American surgeon was at his bedside.

Dad's Ghost--- I knew I was dying the day we left for Houston.

Orlando--- Why did you have to die so young?

Dad's Ghost--- Only God knows your last day on earth.

Mom's Ghost--- *Nadie se muere la víspera* (No one dies on the eve.)

Orlando--- We could not stand your pain, the screams, the suffering. I heard you through the bedroom wall separating your bed from mine.

Dad's Ghost--- My pain was severe. Morphine became my best friend.

Orlando--- What about your soul?

Dad's Ghost--- I had Jesus Christ in my heart. No fear of losing my life, but absolute certainty of my salvation. I expunged all my sins and kept a determined resolve to die in peace with our Lord.

Humberto's Ghost--- It was hell, suffering his torment in parallel with the fear of knowing I was now responsible for all financial needs of the family.

Mom's Ghost--- *Para mí, el sufrimiento fué profundo y duradero.* (For me, suffering was profound and long-lasting.) *Estaba físicamente agotada después de seis meses de noches de insomnio y días terribles.* (I was physically exhausted after six months of sleepless nights and dreadful days.)
Orlando--- Mom.

His suffering was directly transferred to Mother. Those of us who were around at the time, saw the dying differently--close and personal we saw the man, not the condition. Those who loved him from afar, physically detached, saw the condition as a terminal event, remembering and imagining the man they knew so well and sincerely admired.

Mom's Ghost--- *Olía su cuerpo en descomposición mientras cada órgano le fallaba. Él compartió mi dolor al sentir su finalidad. La tristeza era abrumadora, pero tuve que contener las lágrimas y llorar en silencio* (I smelled his decomposing body as each organ failed him. He shared my pain as I sensed his finality. The sadness was overwhelming, but I had to hold back tears and cry in silence.)
Dad's Ghost--- *Tenía miedo, pero alzaste mi determinación de abrazar a Jesús, fortaleciste mi fé y me abrazaste sujetando mi mano.* (I was scared, but you lifted my resolve to embrace Jesus, you strengthened my faith and held my hand while hugging me.)

Our faith moved mountains. Our culture and social comport allowed us to behave with dignity without isolation or shame.

Cubans like to make small talk and mingle, make light of darkness; *"hacer de tripas corazón"* (making heart from tripe.) However, fundamental questions about existence, knowledge, values, reason, mind, and wisdom no longer mattered as much after my father passed. Only the spirit seemed relevant. Philosophical arguments, current and future events and plans became irrelevant. The certainty of death's imagery set a dense overcast covering reasonable thoughts. The heaviness in our hearts foresaw the torment that would follow his terminal illness.

My father died at age forty-two in Madrid, Spain, making mother a widow for the next forty-three years until her death in Pensacola, Florida at age eighty-five. Nevertheless, they enjoyed a relatively short, twenty-year romance in Havana, Miami, and Madrid. Teeming with love and respect, and also pain and tears, as well as joy and happiness, Mother missed him every day for the rest of her life, often bringing his name up for storytelling.

Dad's death meant that I could not see him or speak to him, nor touch him, nor feel his physical presence nearby ever again. It meant that, even though he is far away, he is in my heart, in my thoughts, and in my life. I often pause whatever I am doing to grab a memory from our time together. I am certain that he is doing likewise, looking over my shoulder, pushing me softly over each hurdle life places in my journey.

The tragedy of living is knowing that one day will come when those you love and have loved you back will no longer be around, especially when you may really need them. In my case, our father-son relationship was so pure and whole, so inspiring and educational, so human and warm, and so amazingly beautiful, that his footprint in the sand left beside me as I walk on the beach, provides all the confidence I need to feel blessed.

Orlando--- Good night, Dad.
Dad's Ghost--- Good night, Superboy.

Chapter 29

Return to Flamingo Park

A few years ago, my daughter, Carolina, and her husband, Vivek Jayaram, moved to Miami Beach, FL. Shortly thereafter, they registered their son, Rafa in Baseball at Flamingo Park. I am at the park to see my grandson play. Strong winds blunt reception of sound waves in my iPhone's "voice recorder" application. It is not easy recording playful conversation among parents, sitting in the bleachers at a windy baseball field; coaches yelling instructions to players, and children screaming at themselves and each other.

I could hardly make out words and sounds of encouragement and cheers, muttered non-stop from parents as well as coaches; intended to uplift their children playing T-Ball. The field is well known to me, Flamingo Park, my old playground in South Beach (SOBE).

Orlando--- Hey, Humberto. It's great Dad and Mom chose to move here. What a great idea it was to settle down in such a great place shortly after coming to the US.

Humberto's Ghost---Yes, I remember when we arrived at 24 Espanola Way; our house backed up to the park.

Orlando--- A short jump over a chain-linked fence and we hit the ground running.

Humberto's Ghost--- An old house, a bit small for a family of six but enough to live comfortably.

Orlando--- I know, we enjoyed being so close to the park, and the school.

Humberto's Ghost--- Remember? we played flag football, baseball, and went swimming.

Orlando--- Amazing pool, like the one at Miramar.

Humberto's Ghost--- Remember Ida M. Fisher?

Orlando--- What?

Humberto's Ghost--- The school we attended.

Orlando--- Two blocks from home.

Humberto's Ghost--- What are you doing in Flamingo Park?

Orlando--- We brought Rafa to play baseball.

Humberto's Ghost--- Who is Rafa?

Orlando--- Vivek's first-born.

Humberto's Ghost--- Who is Vivek?

Orlando--- Carolina's husband. They have a little fatty devil we call "el Gordo" but his name is Roman.

Humberto's Ghost--- I like that name.

Orlando--- You always dreamed your boys would be emperors.

Humberto's Ghost--- You are right; you are not the only dreamer amongst us.

Orlando--- I was reminiscing the times we played Little League Baseball.

Humberto's Ghost--- Sixty years ago.

Orlando--- A lifetime.

Sadly, it truly was a lifetime for him, his death coming on Thanksgiving 2007, at the age of sixty-two. Vivek is speaking with Monica, the coach's wife. The coach, Luis has been volunteering for the City of Miami Beach Parks and Recreation Department for several years, in support of his love for baseball.

Orlando--- Luis' father went to school in mid-Beach at St Patrick's Catholic.

Humberto's Ghost--- Did you ask him about Bob Dowling? If I were there, I would ask him about Dowling.

Orlando--- He was a beast.

Humberto's Ghost--- No one in town could steal second base when he was behind the plate. A power hitter, he hit a home run every other game.

Orlando--- We only lost three games under coach Bertman.

Humberto's Ghost--- Yea, Skip was the best.

Coach Bertman (Skip) led the LSU Tigers baseball team to five College World Series championships and seven Southeastern Conference (SEC) championships in eighteen years as head coach.

Orlando--- You were training for that scholarship you won at UM.

Humberto won a baseball scholarship to play second base for the University of Miami, one of the top-ranked teams in the country.

Orlando --- Monica, your father, went to St. Patrick's?

Monica is Luis's wife.

Monica --- No, that was Luis's father.

Laughter, giggling, sighs, and more giggling from the field. All children having lots of fun; the players, as well as the parents, are watching their little boys playing in "real" uniforms; sponsor's name embroidered on the back. The league is organized and run by the city. All coaches are also umpiring. It's the bottom of the third inning.

Vivek--- What's the score?

Monica--- I am not sure. I think they have scored five runs.

Luis--- Yes, it's eleven to five. We are winning.

Whispering into the iPhone, so that others will not notice I was recording, felt weird.

Parent--- C'mon Joey, look at the ball! Do not look away from it! Hit it! Run to first base!

Parent--- C'mon Tommy! C'mon Kenny, pay attention! Move over to your right! A little bit more! That's it!

Vivek--- Rafa is up! RAFA!! Watch the pitcher's hand holding the ball! Look at it, it's leaving his hand! Keep your eyes on it! heh heh.

Orlando--- How long have you guys been doing this?

Monica--- About three years. Right Luis?

Luis--- That's right.

Orlando— What are the ages for "T-Ball?"

Monica--- Four to seven. Then, after that, "Coach Pitch."

Orlando--- Is that eight to ten?

Rafa reached first base, stole second, and the next batter brought him home with a double.

Now on defense, Rafa has his eyes wondering around the field. The ball is hit to the pitcher, bouncing off his leg towards Rafa playing third base. Rafa picks it up, fumbles it, then picks it up again; turns around, runs to third to tag the runner, and steps on the base but gets there too late. Everybody is safe.

Now to the bottom part of the last inning. Rafa hits a double, then moves on to third with the next hitter's single. I am the third base coach.

Orlando--- Rafa, what are you going to do now? Are you watching the pitcher or the batter?

Rafa--- What do you mean, Abo?

Orlando--- What will you do when the batter hits the ball? Pay attention! You must run home the moment you hear the bat hit the ball.

Rafa lifts his eyes to look at me. The bat hits the ball as I was finishing my instructional pep talk. Now, Now, Run, Run!!!

Rafa scores, again. He has crossed the plate three times... a bunch of kids in baseball uniforms playing around having fun.

Then, it hit me.

I was here before.

Afterword

In this work, I often begin each chapter with the tale of my childhood from my mother's perspective. No doubt, she heavily influenced my writing. You already know her name, and all the other characters, and the comments about God, faith, relationships, and chasing ghosts; politics; our love for music and sports; the triple personality; brotherly connectivity; attachments and detachments; death, grief, and forgiveness; anger and abuse; the need for boundaries; immigration, slavery, and racism; friendship and betrayal, disloyalty and consequent trauma from falling victim to falseness, duplicity, and deception; changing from one lifestyle to another, and moving to and from different countries; language, and culture; social psychology; winning and losing; family dependence, connections, and dysfunctional behavior; all through both the pain and joy of living.

This is my story. A Cuban boy looking for and finding his superhero: himself.

References

1. **Superboy and Superman:** Wikipedia contributors. (2021, July 24). Superman. In Wikipedia, The Free Encyclopedia. Retrieved 21:43, July 24, 2021, from Wikipedia contributors. (2021, April 19). **...Preface (page i)**

2. **Family**: Wikipedia contributors. (2021, July 22). Family. In Wikipedia, The Free Encyclopedia. Retrieved 22:09, July 25, 2021, from Wikipedia contributors. (2021, April 19). History of Santería. In *Wikipedia, The Free Encyclopedia*. Retrieved 16:55, September 30, 2021, from https://en.wikipedia.org/w/index.php?title=History_of_Santer%C3%ADa&oldid=1018696306 **...Preface (page i)**

3. **Codependent Attachment:** Codependent Attachment. Psychology Today. Wikipedia contributors. (2021, April 19). History of Santería. In *Wikipedia, The Free Encyclopedia*. Retrieved 16:55, September 30, 2021, from https://en.wikipedia.org/w/index.php?title=History_of_Santer%C3%ADa&oldid=1018696306 **...Chapter 5 (page 28)**

4. **The American Revolution:** Wikipedia contributors. (2021, July 9). American Revolution. In Wikipedia, The Free Encyclopedia. Retrieved 21:41, July 24, 2021, from Wikipedia contributors. (2021, April 19). History of Santería. In *Wikipedia, The Free Encyclopedia*. Retrieved 16:55, September 30, 2021, from https://en.wikipedia.org/w/index.php?title=History_of_Santer%C3%ADa&oldid=1018696306 **...Chapter 6 (page 33)**

5. **The United States Declaration of Independence**: Wikipedia contributors. (2021, July 22). United States Declaration of Independence. In Wikipedia, The Free Encyclopedia. Retrieved 21:40, July 24, 2021 from Wikipedia contributors. (2021, April 19). History of Santería. In *Wikipedia, The Free Encyclopedia*. Retrieved 16:55, September 30, 2021, from https://en.wikipedia.org/w/index.php?title=History_of_Santer%C3%ADa&oldid=1018696306 **...Chapter 6 (page 33)**

6. **Cuba's Declaration of Independence**: Wikipedia contributors. (2021, September 19). History of Cuba. In *Wikipedia, The Free Encyclopedia*. Retrieved 16:22, September 30, 2021, from https://en.wikipedia.org/w/index.php?title=History_of_Cuba&oldid=1045163047 **...Chapter 6 (page 33)**

7. **Cuba's War of Independence:** Wikipedia contributors. (2021, September 12). Cuban War of Independence. In *Wikipedia, The Free Encyclopedia*. Retrieved 16:29, September 30, 2021, from Wikipedia contributors. (2021, April 19). History of Santería. In *Wikipedia, The Free Encyclopedia*. Retrieved 16:55, September 30, 2021, from https://en.wikipedia.org/w/index.php?title=History_of_Santer%C3%ADa&oldid=1018696306 **...Chapter 6 (page 33)**

8. **Jose Marti:** Wikipedia contributors. (2021, April 19). History of Santería. In *Wikipedia, The Free Encyclopedia*. Retrieved 16:55, September 30, 2021, from https://en.wikipedia.org/w/index.php?title=History_of_Santer%C3%ADa&oldid=1018696306https://

digitalcommons.unl.edu/journalismstudent/22 **...Chapter 6 (page 33)**

9. **Cuba's 1902 Constitution:** Wikipedia contributors. (2021, September 28). Cuba. In *Wikipedia, The Free Encyclopedia*. Retrieved 16:41, September 30, 2021, from Wikipedia contributors. (2021, April 19). History of Santería. In *Wikipedia, The Free Encyclopedia*. Retrieved 16:55, September 30, 2021, from https://en.wikipedia.org/w/index.php?title=History_of_Santer%C3%ADa&oldid=1018696306 **...Chapter 6 (page** 34)

10. **Nazi Germany:** Wikipedia contributors. (2021, July 22). Nazi Germany. In Wikipedia, The Free Encyclopedia. Retrieved 21:38, July 24, 2021, from Wikipedia contributors. (2021, April 19). History of Santería. In *Wikipedia, The Free Encyclopedia*. Retrieved 16:55, September 30, 2021, from https://en.wikipedia.org/w/index.php?title=History_of_Santer%C3%ADa&oldid=1018696306 **...Chapter 6 (page 36)**

11. **Sargent's Revolt:** Wikipedia contributors. (2019, December 29). Sergeants' Revolt. In Wikipedia, The Free Encyclopedia. Retrieved 21:37, July 24, 2021, from Wikipedia contributors. (2021, April 19). History of Santería. In *Wikipedia, The Free Encyclopedia*. Retrieved 16:55, September 30, 2021, from https://en.wikipedia.org/w/index.php?title=History_of_Santer%C3%ADa&oldid=1018696306 **...Chapter 6 (page 36)**

12. **Constitution of Cuba:** Wikipedia contributors. (2021, June 5). 1940 Constitution of Cuba. In Wikipedia, The Free Encyclopedia. Retrieved 21:50, July 24, 2021, from Wikipedia contributors. (2021, April 19). History of Santería. In *Wikipedia, The Free Encyclopedia*. Retrieved 16:55, September 30, 2021, from https:// en.wikipedia.org/w/index.php?title=History_of_ Santer%C3%ADa&oldid=1018696306 **...Chapter 6 (page 37)**

13. **Fulgencio Batista:** Wikipedia contributors. (2021, July 21). Fulgencio Batista. In Wikipedia, The Free Encyclopedia. Retrieved 21:55, July 24, 2021 from Wikipedia contributors. (2021, April 19). History of Santería. In *Wikipedia, The Free Encyclopedia*. Retrieved 16:55, September 30, 2021, from https:// en.wikipedia.org/w/index.php?title=History_of_ Santer%C3%ADa&oldid=1018696306 **...Chapter 6 (page 37)**

14. **Santeria and Cuban Folklore:** Wikipedia contributors. (2021, April 19). History of Santería. In *Wikipedia, The Free Encyclopedia*. Retrieved 16:55, September 30, 2021, from Wikipedia contributors. (2021, April 19). History of Santería. In *Wikipedia, The Free Encyclopedia*. Retrieved 16:55, September 30, 2021 from https:// en.wikipedia.org/w/index.php?title=History_of_ Santer%C3%ADa&oldid=1018696306 **...Chapter 6 (page 37)**

15. **Understanding Codependency:** What Codependency Is, and What It Isn't | Psychology Today https://www. psychologytoday.com/us/blog/healthyconnections/201507/ what-codependency-is-andwhat-it-isn **...Chapter 10 (page 81)**

16. **Eric Berne:** Wikipedia contributors. (2021, June 8). Eric Berne. In Wikipedia, The Free Encyclopedia. Retrieved 22:05, July 24, 2021, from https://en.wikipedia.org/w/index.php?title=Eric_Berne&oldid=1027608800 **...Chapter 11 (page 92)**

17. **Alfred E. Neuman:** Wikipedia contributors. (2021, July 11). Alfred E. Neuman. In Wikipedia, The Free Encyclopedia. Retrieved 23:29, July 24, 2021, from https://en.wikipedia.org/w/index.php?title=Alfred_E._Neuman&oldid=1033040535 **...Chapter 11 (page 94)**

18. **Landmark Worldwide:** Wikipedia contributors. (2021, July 24). Landmark Worldwide. In Wikipedia, The Free Encyclopedia. Retrieved 23:32, July 24, 2021, **Chapter 11 (page 99)**

19. **Miramar Yacht Club:** Miramar Yacht Club, Cuba. Miramar Yacht Club Ernestico Martín to .© 2000 - 2012 MYC. Last revised January 22, 2015. **...Chapter 12 (page 103)**

20. **Culver Military Academy:** Culver Summer Camp. https://www.culver.org/summer/camps-available/woodcraft-camp **...Chapter 14 (page 115)**

21. **Juan Manuel Fangio:** Wikipedia contributors. (2021, July 21). Juan Manuel Fangio. In Wikipedia, The Free Encyclopedia. Retrieved 10:53, July 25, 2021, from https://en.wikipedia.org/w/index.php?title=Juan_Manuel_Fangio&oldid=1034627082 **...Chapter 15 (page 133)**

22. **Graham Eckes School:** Palm Beach history: Graham-Eckes School. https:// www.palmbeachdailynews.com/lifestyle/ **...Chapter 16 (page 135)**

23. **The Last Ferry to Freedom:** 1960's Footage Shows The Last Ferry Departing Cuba For The USA https://www.nbcnews.com/video/1960sfootage-shows **...Chapter 18 (page 155)**

24. **Los Milicianos, 26ᵗʰ of July Movement:** Wikipedia contributors. (2021, July 20). 26th of July Movement. In Wikipedia, The Free Encyclopedia. Retrieved 22:02, July 24, 2021, from https://en.wikipedia.org/w/index.php?title=26th_of_July_ Movement&oldid=1034610098 **...Chapter 19 (page 163)**

25. **Committees for the Defense of the Revolution:** In Wikipedia, The Free Encyclopedia. Retrieved 11:51, July 25, 2021, from https://en.wikipedia.org/w/index.php?title=Committees_for_the_Defence_of_the_ Revolution&oldid=1022180159 **...Chapter 19 (page 165)**

26. **Operation Peter Pan:** Wikipedia contributors. (2021, May 31). Operation Peter Pan. In Wikipedia, The Free Encyclopedia. Retrieved 12:00, July 25, 2021, from https://en.wikipedia.org/w/ index.php?title=Operation_Peter_Pan&oldid=1026170908 **...Chapter 19 (page 166)**

27. **Wynwood:** Wikipedia contributors. (2021, June 26). Wynwood. In Wikipedia, The Free Encyclopedia. Retrieved 12:06, July 25, 2021, from https://en.wikipedia.org/w/index. php?title=Wynwood&oldid=1030573668 **...Chapter 19 (page 168)**

28. **Jorge Duany:** Wikipedia contributors. (2021, July 13). Jorge Duany. In Wikipedia, The Free Encyclopedia. Retrieved 12:08, July 25, 2021, from https://en.wikipedia.org/w/index. php?title=Jorge_Duany&oldid=1033460761 **...Chapter 19 (page 169)**

29. **The Day The Music Died:** Wikipedia contributors. (2021, July 21). The Day the Music Died. In Wikipedia, The Free Encyclopedia. Retrieved 12:37, July 25, 2021, from https://en.wikipedia. org/w/index.php?title=The_Day_the_Music_Died&oldid=1034653067 **...Chapter 20 (page 174)**

30. **Flamingo Park:** Wikipedia contributors. (2021, January 6). Flamingo Field. In Wikipedia, The Free Encyclopedia. Retrieved 12:51, July 25, 2021, from https://en.wikipedia. org/w/ index.php?title=Flamingo_Field&oldid=998588660 **...Chapter 21 (page 183)**

31. **Miami Beach, Florida:** Wikipedia contributors. (2021, July 23). Miami Beach, Florida. In Wikipedia, The Free Encyclopedia. Retrieved 00:28, July 26, 2021, from https://en.wikipedia.org/w/index.php?title=Miami_Beach,_Florida&oldid=1035034501 **...Chapter21 (page 183)**

32. **Brigade 2506:** Wikipedia contributors. (2021, July 15). Brigade 2506. In Wikipedia, The Free Encyclopedia. Retrieved 13:10, July 25, 2021, from https://en.wikipedia. org/w/index. php?title=Brigade_2506&oldid=1033763714 **...Chapter 21 (page 185)**

33. **Ashkenazi Jews:** Wikipedia contributors. (2021, July 19). Ashkenazi Jews. In Wikipedia, The Free Encyclopedia. Retrieved 13:09, July 25, 2021, from https://en.wikipedia. org/w/index.php?title=Ashkenazi_Jews&oldid=1034380033 **...Chapter 21 (page 185)**

34. **MBSHS:** Wikipedia contributors. (2021, June 29). Miami Beach Senior High School. In Wikipedia, The Free Encyclopedia. Retrieved 13:13, July 25, 2021, from https://en.wikipedia.org/w/index.php?title=Miami_Beach_Senior_High_ School&oldid=1030971530 **...Chapter 22 (page 187)**

35. **Critical Thinking:** Wikipedia contributors. (2021, June 5). In Wikipedia, The Free Encyclopedia. Retrieved 21:45, July 24, 2021, from https://en.wikipedia.org/w/index.php?title=Critical_thinking&oldid=1027056587 **...Chapter 25 (pagina 211)**

36. **Roman Catholic:** Wikipedia contributors. (2021, July 9). Roman Catholic (term). In Wikipedia, The Free Encyclopedia. Retrieved 15:08, July 25, 2021, from https://en.wikipedia.org/w/index.php?title=Roman_Catholic_(term)&oldid=1032701273 **...Chapter 25 (page 211)**

37. **Catholic Institution:** Wikipedia contributors. (2021, July 16). Catholic Church. In Wikipedia, The Free Encyclopedia. Retrieved 15:02, July 25, 2021, from https://en.wikipedia.org/w/index.php?title=Catholic_Church&oldid=1033928383 **...Chapter 25 (page 211)**

38. **Los Hermanos de La Salle:** El Exilio de los Hermanos De La Salle. Artículo-Reportaje Andrés Valdespino http://delasallealumni.org/nuestroseducadores/HermanosDelaSalle-Exilio.pdf **...Chapter 19 (page 212)**

39. **El Vedado: (The Vedado).** (2021, May 1). Wikipedia, The free =135195249. Accessed on: 14:03, July 25, 2021 from https://es.wikipedia.org/w/index.php?title=El_Vedado&oldid **...Chapter 25 (page 212)**

40. **Resurrection:** Wikipedia contributors. (2021, June 27). Resurrection. In Wikipedia, The Free Encyclopedia. Retrieved 15:26, July 25, 2021, from https://en.wikipedia.org/w/index.php?title=Resurrection&oldid=1030699222 **...Chapter 25 (page 217)**

41. Thomas Aquinas: Wikipedia contributors. (2021, July 15). Thomas Aquinas. In Wikipedia, The Free Encyclopedia. Retrieved 15:30, July 25, 2021, from https://en.wikipedia.org/w/index.php?title=Thomas_Aquinas&oldid=1033778777 **...Chapter 25 (page 217)**

42. Europe: Wikipedia contributors. (2021, July 21). Europe. In Wikipedia, The Free Encyclopedia. Retrieved 15:49, July 25, 2021, from https://en.wikipedia.org/w/index.php?title=Europe&oldid=1034648021 **...Chapter 25 (page 223)**

43. Madrid: Wikipedia contributors. (2021, July 22). Madrid. In Wikipedia, The Free Encyclopedia. Retrieved 15:33, July 25, 2021, from https://en.wikipedia.org/w/index.php?title=Madrid&oldid=1034869307 **...Chapter 25 (page 223)**

44. Castilian Spanish: Wikipedia contributors. (2021, June 18). Castilian Spanish. In Wikipedia, The Free Encyclopedia. Retrieved 15:36, July 25, 2021, from https://en.wikipedia.org/w/index.php?title=Castilian_Spanish&oldid=1029262965 **...Chapter 25 (page 225)**

45. Museo del Prado: Wikipedia contributors. (2021, June 30). Museo del Prado. In Wikipedia, The Free Encyclopedia. Retrieved 15:38, July 25, 2021, from https://en.wikipedia.org/w/index.php?title=Museo_del_Prado&oldid=1031206752 **...Chapter 25 (page 225)**

46. Parque del Retiro: Wikipedia contributors. (2021, April 29). Parque del Buen Retiro, Madrid. In Wikipedia, The Free Encyclopedia. Retrieved 15:40, July 25, 2021, from https://en.wikipedia.org/w/index.php?title=Parque_del_Buen_Retiro,_ Madrid&oldid=1020546737 **...Chapter 25 (page 225)**

47. **Autonomous University of Madrid:** Wikipedia contributors. (2021, May 27). Autonomous University of Madrid. In Wikipedia, The Free Encyclopedia. Retrieved 15:43, July 25, 2021, from https://en.wikipedia.org/w/index.php?title=Autonomous_University_of_Madrid&oldid=1025438467 **...Chapter 25 (page 228)**

48. **Zaragoza:** Wikipedia contributors. (2021, July 12). Zaragoza. In Wikipedia, The Free Encyclopedia. Retrieved 15:34, July 25, 2021, from https://en.wikipedia.org/w/index.php?title=Zaragoza&oldid=1033247246 **...Chapter 25 (page 229)**

49. **University of Zaragoza:** Wikipedia contributors. (2021, July 16). University of Zaragoza. In Wikipedia, The Free Encyclopedia. Retrieved 15:46, July 25, 2021, from https://en.wikipedia.org/w/index.php?title=University_of_Zaragoza&oldid=1033817066 **...Chapter 25 (page 237)**

50. **Spanish Baseball - King's Cup:** Wikipedia contributors. King's Cup baseball [online]. Wikipedia, The Free Encyclopedia, 2020 [accessed July 25, 2021]. Available in https://es.wikipedia.org/w/index.php?title=Copa_del_Rey_de_b%C3%A9baseball&oldid=124664546 **...Chapter 28 (page 243)**

Acknowledgements

With the addition of Dad and Humberto, women influenced me most. During my first fourteen years, there were three: my mother, my grandmother, Esperanza, and my aunt, Chely---Tia Tá. Fifteen thorough eighteen years, Madeline was the most important; at nineteen, Mary Carmen became the woman savior of my lost soul for the next half century, or so, until this writing. Other women, my daughter, Carolina, my sister-law, Norma Gómez, and my sister, Ana Maria, also became essential to my happiness.

Blessed and complete, nearing my life term, I feel endowed as recipient of immensely valuable life gifts. My wife, Mary Carmen, and I are the proud parents of two sons, Carlos and Javier and one daughter, Carolina, each, happily embraced in true love and absolute commitment to their wonderful life partners: Cindy (Carlos), Lacy (Javier) and Vivek (Carolina). They have brought the biggest joy we could have ever dreamed owning. Our six grandchildren: Gaston and Carson (Carlos and Cindy), Rafa and Roman (Carolina and Vivek), and Cassius and Joaquin (Javier and Lacy).

Lastly, I must give credit and thanks to God, my Savior and coauthor.

TOGETHER
Over the Years

CPSIA information can be obtained
at www.ICGtesting.com
Printed in the USA
BVHW061601221121
622219BV00010B/540